Rare Old Dublin

First published in 2002 by
Marino Books
an imprint of Mercier Press
16 Hume Street Dublin 2
Tel: (01) 661 5299; Fax: (01) 661 8583
E-mail: books@marino.ie
www.mercierpress.ie

Trade enquiries to CMD Distribution
55A Spruce Avenue
Stillorgan Industrial Park
Blackrock County Dublin
Tel: (01) 294 2560; Fax: (01) 294 2565
E-mail: cmd@columba.ie

© Frank Hopkins 2002

ISBN 1 86023 150 0
10 9 8 7 6 5 4 3 2 1

A CIP record for this title is available
from the British Library

Cover design by Marino Design

Printed by CPD Group
Harmondsworth Middlesex UK

Rare Old Dublin

Heroes, Hawkers & Hoors

Frank Hopkins

for Nóirín, Róisín, Ella and Jack

CONTENTS

Author's Note

I was the product of a mixed Dublin marriage – a northside mother and a southside father. I have forgiven them (after forty years) for the disservice of bringing me into the world as a little Englishman. Thankfully, I was rescued and repatriated at an early age. *Rare Old Birmingham* doesn't have quite the same ring.

If I had been left to my own devices, this book would never have happened. I owe thanks to Frank Coughlan for cultivating the germ of an idea; Sean McConnell for coming up with the title of the book; and Jo O'Donoghue and her team at Marino Books for their professionalism and patience.

I'm grateful to the staff of the National Library of Ireland and the National Archives for their assistance. Thanks also to the team at the *Evening Herald* for their support – especially Declan Cahill and Ronan Price. The pieces in this book were first published in my column, Cityscapes, in the *Evening Herald*.

On a personal level I'd like to thank Sean McConnell and Kieran O'Brien – two hoors who became friends – for their inspiration and encouragement on many long days spent in the Dublin and Wicklow mountains.

Finally I'd like to thank my partner-in-crime Nóirín Hegarty for her sometimes provocative but always encouraging insights into the work-in-progress.

BULLY'S ACRE

The Royal Hospital in Kilmainham was built between 1680 and 1687 for the reception of aged and infirm British army pensioners. It was designed by the Irish Surveyor-General, William Robinson, who was heavily influenced by the *Invalides* military hospital in Paris, built by Louis XIV. Just inside the Kilmainham gate of the hospital is Dublin's oldest cemetery. It was at one time known as the Hospital Fields, but more recently as Bully's Acre. It is not known who or what the graveyard is named after, but one explanation advanced in the past suggests that the name is a corruption of 'bailly' or 'bailiff'.

During the middle of the eighteenth century, General Dilks, a Master of the Royal Hospital, walled the cemetery, demolished the graves and headstones and tried to have the cemetery converted into a pleasure garden. He went too far, however, when he attempted to cut off access to the graveyard altogether by erecting a large gate across a traditional right of way known as Lord Galway's Walk. Bully's Acre was the only free burial place for the city's poor, and Dubliners, who had been burying their dead at Bully's Acre for centuries, tore down all the walls at the cemetery after a judge ruled that the gate was to be removed.

Bully's Acre continued to be used as a public graveyard until its closure during the great cholera epidemic of 1832. It has been claimed that over three thousand burials took place there during a six-month period that year, with five hundred victims being buried in ten days at the height of the epidemic.

11

The authorities were forced to close the cemetery down due to overcrowding.

Popular tradition tells us that Brian Ború camped near the site of the cemetery on the eve of the Battle of Clontarf, and it is said that his son Murrough and grandson Turlough, killed during the battle, are buried there. Another person of renown to be interred at Bully's Acre – at least temporarily – was Robert Emmet. It appears that he was initially buried at Bully's Acre but that soon afterwards his remains were taken to an as-yet-unknown location.

Seventeen years later, in 1820, the Dublin-born boxing legend Dan Donnelly was buried at Bully's Acre. Thousands of mourners followed the funeral cortège and Donnelly's gloves were carried at the head of the procession on a silk cushion. Some of the mourners unhitched the horses from the hearse and pulled it themselves out to Kilmainham. Soon afterwards, in an incident that led to outrage in Dublin, Donnelly's remains were dug up by medical students, who sold them to a surgeon named Hall. The surgeon removed the corpse's right arm and returned the rest of the body for reburial. The arm was last seen quite recently, on display in the Hideout pub in Kilcullen, County Kildare.

It appears that Dan Donnelly was not the only victim of the body-snatchers. Judging by a report published in the *Lancet* in 1830, Bully's Acre provided many corpses for the students of the Dublin medical schools: 'An abundant supply is obtained for all the Dublin Schools from the burying ground known as the Bully's Acre. There is no watch on this ground and subjects are to be got with great facility.'

THE THINGMOTE

Right up until the end of the seventeenth century, an unusual Viking monument stood in an area bounded by College Green, Suffolk Street and Church Lane. The monument – known as the 'Thingmote' – was cone-shaped and featured terracing. It was forty feet high and two hundred and forty feet in circumference. 'Thingmote' was a Norse phrase that translates roughly as 'people mound'. Thingmotes were not an exclusively Dublin phenomenon and were found in other parts of the Viking kingdom, such as the Orkney Islands and the Isle of Man. This was the place where the Norsemen customarily held their assemblies, passed laws and held sporting tournaments. It is also possible that they used the mound for darker purposes. There is some evidence to suggest that the Thingmote was used for ritual sacrifices to the Norse gods Thor and Odin. These ritual sacrifices involved breaking the sacrificial victims' backs by dropping large stones on them.

Non-sacrificial killings were also carried out, but not at the Thingmote. The Norse custom was that common-or-garden executions should take place some distance away. It was ordained that the killing ground should contain – according to Halliday's *Scandinavian Kingdom of Dublin* – 'a stony hill, where there should be neither arable land nor green fields'. The spot chosen by the Dublin Vikings for this purpose was an area between Lower Baggot Street and Lower Pembroke Street. It was called the '*Hangr Hoeg*'. This place fulfilled all the above criteria as it was located on a stony hill and nothing grew on the barren ground surrounding it.

It was at the Thingmote that Henry II tried to win over the Gaelic chieftains at Christmas in 1172, after the Anglo-Norman invasion. Henry ordered a wickerwork palace to be constructed, after the Gaelic fashion. He realised that the Irish kings were used to taking part in Norse festivities at the Thingmote and he hoped that they could be wooed by being offered some Norman hospitality. Giraldus Cambrensis mentions in his *Conquest of Ireland* that the kings attending the feast 'began to eat the flesh of the crane, which they had hitherto loathed'.

In 1487, the Earl of Kildare – Gearóid Mór – had a messenger from the Mayor of Waterford hanged at the Thingmote for delivering the message that the citizens of Waterford would not support the cause of the pretender to the English throne, Lambert Simnel.

The Thingmote was demolished in the late seventeenth century by William Davis, the City Recorder and Chief Justice. The land on which the mound stood was very valuable and he wanted to extend one of his properties next to the mound. He had the Thingmote taken down and the earth was used to help raise the level of Patrick's Well Lane (now Nassau Street). In May 1857, when work was being carried out in Suffolk Street, workmen discovered a cist grave containing the crouched skeleton of a man and two copper axeheads. The find was subsequently dated to 1800 BC. This led to speculation that the Norsemen built their Thingmote over an existing monument belonging to a much earlier period. In addition to utilising the physical material of the mound, it is also possible that they took over an existing ceremonial site used by previous generations of Irish people.

THE HELLFIRE CLUB

The Hellfire Club is one of the city's best-known landmarks. It was built in 1725, on the summit of Mount Pelier in the Dublin Mountains, by William 'Speaker' Connolly, possibly for use as a hunting lodge. The building was constructed on the site of a prehistoric burial cairn and some of the granite stones surrounding the tomb were used in the construction.

It hadn't been long built when, during the course of a terrible storm, the roof was blown off. At the time, local people believed that the devil had caused the destruction of the roof because of the desecration of the cairn. Connolly replaced the roof with a reinforced arched structure that is still in place today.

The building was known as the Hellfire Club because it was used by a group of wealthy members of the ruling classes who liked to think of themselves as 'bucks' or 'rakes'. These 'gentlemen' were dedicated to drink, duelling, dice and debauchery of every kind. The Hellfire Club was established in 1735 by the first Earl of Rosse, Richard Parsons. Other members included Jack St Leger, who was so taken with the Duchess of Rutland that he used to drink her used bathwater; a Dublin sheriff called Simon Luttrell; and Richard Chapel Whaley. Whaley was known as 'Burn Chapel' because he had burnt down a Catholic church while engaged in a priest-hunting expedition.

The club was modelled on similar fraternities in England and the members usually met at the Eagle Tavern or Lucas's Coffee House on Cork Hill near Christchurch. On occasion, dressed in their uniform of red cloaks and white socks, the club would ride out to Mount Pelier for long nights of revelry, drinking vast quantities of a concoction made from whiskey and butter known as 'scaltheen'.

There are many strange tales associated with the Hellfire Club, including black magic, ritual sacrifice and card-playing with the devil. The latter is the most popular tale and usually involves the devil accidentally revealing his cloven hoof at the card table and then vanishing, screaming, up the chimney.

Another tale concerns the above-mentioned Richard 'Burn Chapel' Whaley. It seems that during a Black Mass, a servant slipped and spilled a drink on Whaley's coat while attempting to make his way over the bodies of fallen drunkards. The enraged Whaley doused the servant in brandy and set him and the lodge on fire.

There are other popular Hellfire Club legends concerning the ritual sacrifice of black cats. One of these tales relates how a priest interrupted a ceremony in which a large black cat was being sacrificed. The priest burst into the room, laid his hands on the cat and uttered a prayer. The cat exploded and revealed itself to be a demon, which hurtled through the roof. Another horrific tale relates to a black cat being dipped in scaltheen, set on fire and thrown from a window of the Hellfire Club.

At some of their gatherings, a large black cat would be given pride of place at the head of the table. This cat, representing the devil, was given precedence over the entire gathering and usually sat beside the chairman at meetings.

After Richard Parsons' death in 1741, the Hellfire Club appears to have been disbanded. As he lay dying at his home in Molesworth Street, a neighbouring vicar sent him a letter urging him to repent for his life of wickedness. With great amusement, Parsons, noticing that the letter was addressed 'My Lord', resealed it and had it delivered to Lord Kildare, who was, as John Gilbert put it, 'one of the most pious noblemen of the age, and in every respect a contrast in character to Lord Rosse'. Parsons died leaving the unfortunate vicar trying to explain his actions to the archbishop. When the truth eventually emerged, Parsons was already on his way to a better – and presumably much hotter – place.

Coburg Gardens

Often described as one of Dublin's best-kept secrets, the Iveagh Gardens, just behind the National Concert Hall, have a long and diverse history. The gardens in their present form were laid out in 1863 by Benjamin Lee Guinness after he had built Iveagh House on St Stephen's Green. The grounds – still in the process of restoration – were developed by the famous garden designer Ninian Niven, and many of the original features can still be seen today. These include a cascade, fountains, a maze and a rose garden. Another unusual feature is the long sunken lawn just inside the Clonmel Street gate, which was designed for archery competitions.

The area was originally set out as a private pleasure garden by 'Copper-faced Jack', Earl of Clonmel, behind his house on Harcourt Street. Jack was often seen emerging from an underground passage that connected his house to the gardens on his way to consult with his Stephen's Green neighbour Francis Higgins, 'the Sham Squire'.

During the early nineteenth century, the gardens were thrown open to the public and were called the Coburg Gardens after the family of Saxe-Coburg, who were related to Queen Victoria's mother. During that time, the gardens were a popular place of amusement for fashionable Dublin society and many concerts and exhibitions were held there. Attractions at the gardens were usually advertised in the Dublin newspapers of the day. One such advertisement in June 1828 announced details of a spectacular fireworks display organised by a Monsieur Piron, a famed pyrotechnist from the Tivoli Gardens in Paris. Large crowds were expected to view the spectacle and a strong military detachment was deployed to keep gatecrashers at bay. Despite the elaborate preparations for the event, it was postponed for three days due to exceptionally heavy rain.

Another fireworks display was held at the gardens to celebrate a victory of the British navy over the Turkish fleet; five replica Turkish frigates were burned in the park. Once again, a large force of soldiers was stationed around the gardens to keep the lower orders away from the event 'so that ladies need not apprehend the least inconvenience from the presence of a crowd.'

The Coburg Gardens provided the setting for a major riot in August 1835, during which several Orangemen were badly injured. During a trade union meeting in the park, organised by Thomas Reynolds, the mainly Catholic coal-porters, bricklayers and brewers' draymen in the crowd attacked a hundred and fifty Orangemen with what were described in a later court report as 'murderous instruments of aggression'. Dozens of Orangemen were carried away injured, while another six or seven had to be taken to nearby hospitals. The riot spilled over into Stephen's Green and Grafton Street, and all the windows in the Merchant's Hall were smashed. Reynolds was later charged and convicted of assault, riotous assembly and breach of the peace, for which he was sentenced to nine months' imprisonment.

The Coburg Gardens fell into disuse until 1860, when they were purchased and restored to order by Benjamin Lee Guinness. The park seems to have been used as a municipal rubbish dump during the intervening years. One writer described the park as having 'heaps of rubbish thrown into it' and as a place 'where only sheep were allowed to graze'.

The Ghost of Belvedere House

Great Denmark Street, which was once part of Gardiner Row, is believed to have been named after the Queen of Denmark, sister of George III, who died in 1775. This had been a semi-rural area until the 1770s, when several townhouses were built there to accommodate the nobility and landed gentry.

In his book *North Dublin, City and County*, Dillon Cosgrave mentions a private school run by the Rev George Wright at 2 Great Denmark Street that was attended by the novelist Charles Lever. Cosgrave relates a battle that occurred between students at Wright's school and pupils of another private school at Grenville Street. During the course of the 'mill', which took place at a spot called 'Mountjoy's Fields', the Denmark Street boys exploded a mine, injuring many on both sides. The ringleaders – including Lever – were arrested and taken to Marlborough Street police station. Lever was chosen as spokesman for the students; he managed to smooth-talk the magistrate, who let them off with a caution.

Number 3 Great Denmark Street was the home of one Lord Norbury, also known as John 'the Hanging Judge' Toler. Norbury was one of the most corrupt judges the country has ever seen. He was eventually removed from the bench in 1827 due to his absent-mindedness and his inclination to fall asleep during important trials. Lord Norbury died at his home on 27 July 1831 at the age of eighty-five and was buried at St Mary's Church, Mary Street, Dublin. While on his deathbed, he learned that his neighbour Lord Erne was also near death. Allegedly he called to his servant and said, 'James, run around to Lord Erne and tell him with my compliments that it will be a dead heat between us.'

Belvedere House at Great Denmark Street was built in 1775 for George Rochfort, the second Earl of Belvedere, who owned a large estate at Gaulstown in Westmeath. It cost the princely sum of £24,000 to construct. This was probably the first house to be built in Denmark Street. The house was sold to the Jesuits in 1841, when it became Belvedere College. They purchased the adjoining property, owned by Lord Fingal, three years later.

Belvedere House is alleged to have been haunted by George Rochfort's mother, Mary Molesworth, the first Lady Belvedere, who is said to have died there. Mary, daughter of Colonel Molesworth, was forced to marry Colonel Rochfort – very much against her will – at the tender age of sixteen in 1736. Ten years into the marriage, Rochfort received an anonymous tip-off that Mary was having an affair with his brother Arthur. Rochfort immediately began a legal action against his brother and was awarded damages of £20,000. Arthur was unable to pay the damages and he fled the country. Rochfort exacted his revenge on his wife by keeping her locked up at their estate at Gaulstown. Although he allowed Mary the freedom of the estate, she was not allowed to step outside the gates of Gaulstown and she remained a prisoner there for seventeen years. She did manage to escape after twelve years but Rochfort took her back to Gaulstown within a day of her flight, after her father, Lord Molesworth, refused her refuge.

On her return to Gaulstown, Mary was kept under closer surveillance by Rochfort and he withdrew many of her privileges. During the last five years of her confinement she was not allowed to see her children or correspond with the outside world. She was also forbidden to engage in any recreational activities. Mary was not released from imprisonment until Rochfort's death in 1772. Although she was only in her early forties, she was said to have the look of a woman twice her age; she spent the remaining years of her life in seclusion.

Riding the Franchises

Picture this scenario if you can! The Lord Mayor of Dublin, decked out in his full mayoral regalia, riding on horseback out to the suburbs to mark the boundaries of the city, closely followed by the leaders of the Dublin trade unions. Sounds far-fetched? Well, maybe in this day and age, but for many hundreds of years, before the advent of Ordnance Survey maps and aerial photography, this was quite a common spectacle for the citizens of Dublin.

The practice of 'riding the franchises' of the city was established in 1192 when King John granted the citizens of Dublin the right 'both within and without the walls there to have their boundaries as perambulated on oath by good men of the city'. It was originally intended that this procession would take place every three years but this didn't always happen.

The procession usually began at Dames' Gate and followed a route that took the participants out past Trinity College via Townsend Street, and then to Ringsend. On reaching the strands beyond Ringsend and Sandymount, it was customary for one of the party to ride into the sea and throw a spear as far out into the water as possible. The party then made its way from Ringsend across the sands to the 'black stone' (Blackrock) and returned to the city via Merrion and Donnybrook. From there, the mayor and his followers made their way to the Coombe, where they sometimes paused for refreshments with the locals.

The party then rode out to Kilmainham and crossed the

Liffey into Stoneybatter. They passed through Cabra and on to Grangegorman, where the ceremonial sword was thrust out of the east window of the old priory to mark the boundary dividing the city from the Prior of Grangegorman's lands. On the final leg of the journey the riders moved on to Glasnevin, Drumcondra and Ballybough before crossing the Tolka river and proceeding to the final stopping point on their journey, just beyond Clontarf. Then it was back to the city, to the Lord Mayor's house, where the party dispersed.

The 'riding of the franchises' from the sixteenth to the late eighteenth century was always a festive occasion and made a great spectacle for the Dublin public. Along with the Lord Mayor, every trade guild in the city was represented in the procession. No expense was spared by the guilds for the event and it was very important to be seen to put on a good show for the day.

Jonah Barrington, in his *Personal Sketches*, written in 1827, leaves us a colourful account of the processions. Barrington didn't give the year for this particular procession but it appears to have been in the late eighteenth century.

> For this procession every member of the twenty-five corporations [guilds] prepared as for a jubilee . . . They borrowed the finest horses and trappings which could be procured; the masters rode, the journeymen walked, and were succeeded by the apprentices.

The procession was similar to the modern St Patrick's Day parade and each guild had its own float. The blacksmiths had a working forge drawn by horses, the skinners and tanners dressed up in goat and sheepskins, while the butchers adorned themselves with cowhides and horns and brandished meat cleavers at the spectators!

By 1787, the 'riding of the franchises' had declined as a

public spectacle due to cost-cutting measures imposed by the corporation and it was replaced by a greatly scaled down version. Barrington described the new ceremony as a 'wretched substitute' which involved the mayor and a 'dozen of dirty constables' riding the boundaries of the city 'in privacy and silence'.

THE BRAZEN HEAD

The Brazen Head on Dublin's Bridge Street is a well-known landmark on Dublin's tourist trail; it has been serving locals since 1613. Although it is widely known as the oldest tavern in Ireland and perhaps even in Europe – the sign over the door maintains that it was founded in 1198 – few people know how it got its famous name.

There are two other public houses of the same name in Ireland but only one has come up with an explanation for its origins. Apparently during the Siege of Limerick a cannon ball was fired by the Williamite army and 'removed the head of a well-known red-haired girl of ill-repute' while she was watching the battle against Sarsfield and his men from the window of the brothel. When a new tavern was built on the site of the house in 1794 it was called 'The Sign of the Brazen Head'.

The first record of ownership of the Brazen Head is made in a court claim against Richard Fagan and his wife Eleanor in 1613 in relation to a fine levied on 'one messuage and garden called the Brazen Head in Bridge Street in the City of Dublin'. The Fagans were landed gentry who owned considerable tracts of land in Dublin, Meath, Sligo and Munster.

In 1703, however, the tavern was granted to a James King, who had made a claim against the fortified estates of Richard Fagan; Fagan had resigned his commission in King James's army and surrendered to King William of Orange after the Battle of the Boyne. Bridge Street at that time was a residential area for wealthy merchants and the gentry and the court papers record that James King was granted 'all that large timber house called the Brazen Head containing 35 feet 6 inches in front, 49 feet in rear and 168 feet in depth with all outhouses, stables, yards etc.' In 1704, despite objections by local traders, King was granted permission by the City Assembly to expand the inn with the lease of a tower and part of the city wall at the back of the Brazen Head. Shortly afterwards it was reported in the newspapers that the Brazen Head had been robbed of goods worth £60.

In 1710 James King was replaced by Robert King as the owner and in 1765 an advertisement in *Faulkner's Dublin Journal* records that a new tenant was being sought for the inn. The tenancy of the thirty-room tavern was granted to Robert Autchinson of Mabbot Street.

Denis Mitchell took over the Brazen Head in 1783 and ran it for thirty-nine years. During his tenure, the name of Oliver Bond – who lived on Bridge Street – and other leaders of the United Irishmen became forever associated with the pub, where they used to hold their meetings. It was in the Brazen Head that Bond outlined his plans for the capture of Dublin and later Robert Emmet reputedly hid out after the rising of 1803. His desk was preserved in the house and one of the rooms is named after him. In later centuries the insurrectionists of 1916 and the leaders of the War of Independence, including Michael Collins, gathered there for meetings to plan revolution.

The Brazen Head was a favourite haunt of Flann O'Brien (Myles na gCopaleen) and Brendan Behan. And James Joyce mentions it in *Ulysses*, when the vagrant Corley tells Stephen Dedalus and Bloom that one can get 'a decent enough do for a bob' there. It's no longer a hotel offering lodgings, and there's nowhere nowadays to keep your horse, but the Brazen Head is still serving good food and drink to Dubliners and tourists alike.

THE GREEN TUREEN MURDER

Few people in Ireland had ever heard of Hazel Mullen or her boyfriend Shan Mohangi when she went missing in the middle of August 1963. But within days, all that was to change. To this day, Dubliners recall the dashing twenty-two-year-old College of Surgeons student who was subsequently convicted of killing sixteen-year-old Hazel.

Mohangi strangled Hazel and cut up her body with a meat cleaver from the kitchen of the Green Tureen restaurant. Seventeen different parts of the young Shankill girl's body were found by police in the basement of 95 Harcourt Street. Knives, cleavers and blood told the horror of what had occurred on Saturday 17 August 1963.

The *Irish Press* of Wednesday 21 August carried a front-page story recounting the events at 95 Harcourt Street, dramatically relating how the owner of the building, Cecil Frew, raised the alarm after Mohangi confessed the killing to him. Sergeant James Connell was the first police officer at the scene and told how he approached the student's flat on the second-floor landing.

'I could see the light was on. I knocked twice and got no reply. Then I smelled the gas and heard it running in the room. We forced the door and when I entered I saw Mohangi lying on a bed apparently asleep. I turned off two gas jets, one on a cooker and one on a gas fire, pulled back the curtains and opened both windows.'

In an attempt to end his own life, Mohangi had taken tablets and tried to gas himself, but he subsequently recovered and on Monday 10 February 1964 he went on trial for Hazel's murder. Sixteen days later, a jury found him guilty and he was sentenced to death. Mohangi immediately appealed against the sentence.

In his statement to gardaí, Mohangi said that he and Hazel had planned to get engaged. He said that on that fateful Saturday she had finished work at Brown's Chemists in Stephen's Green at 12.30 and had arrived at Number 95 for lunch between 1 and 1.05 PM.

'She asked me if she could see the place,' Mohangi said. 'I brought her down and showed her all over the basement. She told me in the basement that she had something to do with somebody else. She did not mention the person's name but she said it was sex.

'I don't know what happened me . . . I was raging at this time. I got hold of her by the neck and put my hands around her neck, and before I knew anything it was the end. I did not intend killing Hazel. The moment I learned she was unfaithful to me I lost my head and did something rash which I am regretting now.'

In January 1965, at a retrial, Mohangi was found guilty of the lesser offence of manslaughter and was sentenced to seven years in jail. He served just three years of his sentence before being deported to South Africa; he now lives in Natal with his wife and three children. He dropped the name Mohangi – which had become so infamous in Ireland – and adopted the name Shan Jamuma, a family name from his mother's side. In 1984 he stood for election to the controversial 'coloured chamber' and won a seat for the Natal province. After the apartheid system crumbled, however, he was unsuccessful when he stood for election for the National Party.

In 1994 he gave an interview to an RTÉ camera crew for the *Thou Shalt Not Kill* series. As he remembered that awful night of thirty years previously, his voice broke and he had difficulty articulating his remorse. 'If I had one wish, it would be to bring Hazel Mullen back and undo what has been done. But that is not possible,' he said.

The Steyne

The earliest surviving Anglo-Norman records make several references to an area outside the old walls of Dublin called the 'Steyne' or 'Stein'. The Steyne district covered an area stretching from Suffolk Street down to the Dodder river and back to where Baggot Street now runs. From 900 AD up to the mid-seventeenth century, it was a well-known and important part of Dublin. The central portion of the district was at the intersection of the present-day Townsend and Hawkins Streets. It must be remembered that the Liffey was not walled in at that time and the sandy shoreline of the river stretched much further back from the river than it does today.

The name of the area evolved from the Vikings' custom of erecting a long stone at their landing places. When they first sailed into Dublin in their longboats, they erected an unmarked stone pillar between twelve and fourteen feet high just above the high-tide mark at Hawkins Street. This type of pillar has also been found near Viking settlements on the Isle of Man and the Orkney Islands. For many years, the shoreline in the vicinity of the Long Stone continued to be used for landing and picking up passengers and was heavily used by the merchants of Dublin.

In 1220 the Priory of All Hallows (where Trinity College now stands) founded a hospice on the lands of the Steyne for the use of lepers intending to visit the shrine of St James of Compostella, who was the patron saint of lepers. According to one source, the lepers were not allowed out of the grounds

31

of the hospital unless they were accompanied by two attendants, one carrying a bell and crying out 'Unclean! Unclean!' and the other carrying a forty-foot pole to keep 'clean' Dubliners out of harm's way.

In 1646, 'noble ladies' who wanted to assist in the fortification of Dublin 'condescended to carry baskets of earth'. In doing so, they managed to destroy an ancient Viking tomb. The tomb was described as containing large quantities of coals, ash and the charred remains of human bones. This monument was situated close to the Long Stone and was in keeping with the Norse custom of burying their leaders near the traditional landing places. It appears from existing Danish and Norwegian records that the body that was dug up could possibly have been that of Ivar, son of Regnar Lodbrok; Ivar ruled over Dublin and died in 872 AD. These records suggest that he asked to be buried near the Long Stone.

The Long Stone disappeared from public view during the latter part of the seventeenth century when William Davis, the City Recorder, was improving his property near St Andrew's Church. He also had the forty-foot-high Viking place of assembly – the Thingmote – demolished for landfill at Nassau Street. The Long Stone was removed and it was last spotted lying against a fence in the grounds of Trinity College.

Priest-catchers

Seventeenth-century Dublin was definitely not the place to be if you happened to be a priest of the 'Romish persuasion'. In 1623 an edict was issued by Dublin Castle ordering the banishment of 'Jesuits, friars and popish priests out of Ireland within forty days'.

During the late seventeenth and early eighteenth centuries, when the Catholic clergy had prices on their heads, the most reviled profession in the city was that of priest-catcher. It was a lucrative business that offered £150 for the capture of an archbishop or bishop and £50 for the taking and conviction of a priest. Curiously, a reward of £200 was on offer for the conviction of any person found guilty of sheltering a bishop in his home.

To the citizens of Dublin – Catholic and Protestant – the priest-catcher was the lowest form of life. Once a priest-catcher had been identified, he could never again walk the streets without grave risk to his life. In 1728, the Protestant Archbishop of Dublin told the Archbishop of Canterbury that it was not uncommon to see mobs of five hundred or six hundred angry Dubliners armed with cudgels and stones in hot pursuit of a priest-catcher.

One of this breed was a Doctor John Molloy, who complained long and hard to the aforementioned Archbishop of Dublin about the beatings he received from the Papists. On one occasion, he was 'outed' by a man called Samuel Dye, who followed him through the streets of Dublin shouting 'Priest-catcher! Priest-catcher!' In no time at all he was fleeing for his life at the head of a baying mob. Molloy managed to survive by hiding in a house.

The most infamous priest-catcher of those times was a Spaniard called John Garzia. Garzia arrived in Dublin in 1717 and immediately set about infiltrating the Catholic community in the city. He posed as a priest and stayed at the Franciscan friary of Adam and Eve on Merchants Quay. The present-day Adam and Eve Church takes its name from the Adam and Eve tavern on Cook Street where the Franciscans once held secret Masses. Catholics posing as drinkers would be admitted by a guard on saying the words: 'I am going to the Adam and Eve.'

A few months later, Garzia made his move. He went to Dublin Castle and handed over information relating to the activities of various priests. Acting on this information, the authorities raided several houses around the city on the morning of 1 June 1718 and rounded up seven clergymen. The haul included Doctor Edmund Byrne, Archbishop of Dublin, and Father Anthony Bryan, who had earlier been parish priest of Rathfarnham.

The bishop and priests were put on trial in November of that year, with Garzia as the star witness. With the exception of the archbishop, the priests were found guilty and sentenced to transportation. It is not known whether this sentence was carried out. England went to war with Spain at Christmas that year and the ships used for transportation were requisitioned by the authorities. It *is* known, however, that priests who had been transported earlier in the year returned under false names and were generally left to go about their work unharmed.

Meanwhile, Garzia was being subjected to the usual treatment reserved for priest-catchers by the citizens of Dublin. In a letter to the Lord Justice, he complained that the mob had 'contrived ways to take away his life'. He mentions one incident in particular in James's Street when he was 'insulted, beat and much abused', barely escaping with his life. Garzia was the last of the official priest-catchers. With the increasing toleration of Catholics by the authorities and constant harassment by the inhabitants of Dublin, Garzia realised that his days were numbered; he left Ireland in 1723.

THE TALKING CROSS

Today, Christchurch Cathedral is a required stop for tourists in Dublin, but its history goes back much further than most of us realise. *The Black Book of Christchurch* tells us that Sitric, son of Olaf, the Norse King of Dublin, was responsible for the construction of the vaults of the present cathedral. In 1038 he gave the church to Donagh, Bishop of Dublin, in honour of the Blessed Trinity.

One hundred and fifty years later, the Welsh chronicler Giraldus Cambrensis documented some 'miracles' associated with Christchurch in his *Topographia Hiberniae*. He described the 'talking cross' at the church and related the tale of how the cross had been asked to intervene in a row between two citizens over money. Apparently, the man who was owed the money asked the marvellous talking cross to bear witness to the contract, and the cross duly obliged!

When Strongbow arrived at Dublin in 1169, the Norsemen attempted to flee in their longboats, taking their crucifix with them, but no amount of force on their part could get the cross to move. After securing the city, Giraldus tells us that a Norman archer with a guilty conscience made an offering of a penny to the cross, but as he walked away, the money was flung at his back. He went back, placed the money at the base of the cross and departed again, with the same result. The archer then publicly confessed to robbing the archbishop's house earlier in the day and gave back his ill-gotten gains. Then, with great humility, he carried the penny back to the cross again and this time the money remained where it was.

The talking cross was held in great esteem and many pilgrims journeyed from far and near to see the marvel for themselves. St Laurence O'Toole was a devotee of the cross and was known to converse with it on occasion. The cross did not seem to get on as well with St Laurence's successor, Bishop John Comyn. For reasons that are unclear, he once ruled that all crucifixes and statues in the church be placed flat on the ground and surrounded with thorns. After six days of lying on the floor, the miraculous cross began, according to a Norman observer, to 'writhe in agony, its face glowing and perspiring as though it had been placed in a fiery furnace.'

Christchurch Cathedral was at one time surrounded by several narrow lanes and alleyways that came right up to its walls. One of these passages, which led to Christchurch yard on the western side of Fishamble Street, was known to locals as 'Hell'. The lane had an arch over which there was a large image of the devil carved in oak. 'Hell' contained many inns and taverns and its fame spread well beyond the confines of Dublin. It had several lodging houses and a newspaper of the day carried a notice advertising 'Apartments in Hell' that would be well suited for a member of the legal profession.

THE JAMES'S STREET WORKHOUSE

In 1704, the Duchess of Ormond laid the foundations for a workhouse at James's Street on the site of the present hospital. It was the first workhouse to be built in the city and could cater for a hundred and sixty people. Those who could work were paid eightpence a day for their labour. Those who were unable to work were subjected to many hardships such as floggings and beatings. Diseased beggars were turned away at the door, along with the disabled. The diet in the workhouse consisted of milk, bread and gruel and a concoction known as 'burgoo', a meal made of water and oats and seasoned with salt and pepper.

The workhouse also accepted orphaned children, and from 1729 until its closure it was used solely for the reception of abandoned children. These babies were known as 'foundlings' and the hospital was thereafter called 'the Dublin Foundling Hospital'. The following year, the infamous 'cradle' was installed at the hospital. The cradle was a constantly turning wheel beside the gates of the hospital; it was used to take in unwanted infants at any time of the day or night. During the 130-year history of the hospital, it was estimated that nearly a quarter of a million abandoned children passed through the cradle.

The hospital was originally set up with two aims in mind. The first was to prevent 'exposure, death and actual murder of illegitimate children', while the second was to rear the children in the Protestant faith and keep them in care until the age of sixteen. Neither of these aims was realised. So many children died during their stay at the hospital that it became the subject of repeated investigations. Between 1750 and 1760, there were 7,781 admissions of children recorded. Nearly 4,000 of these children died in the hospital, while fifty-two were unaccounted for. Even more shocking is the report to an Irish House of Commons subcommittee in 1797. This report revealed that between 1791 and 1796, of the 5,216 children sent to the hospital's infirmary, only one came out alive. During the first three months of 1795, 540 children went in through the gates of the Foundling Hospital and only a hundred survived.

The conditions in which the children were left to die are graphically described in James Collins's book *Life in Old Dublin*. Apparently, the children were brought to the infirmary and were placed 'five and six huddled and crushed together in the receptacles called cradles, swarming with vermin, and they were then covered over with filthy and dirty blankets.'

During the inquiry into the deaths, the committee focused on a feature of the infirmary known as 'the bottle'. This bottle was liberally passed around the children at regular intervals, after which they were 'easy' for several hours afterwards. The hospital surgeon on his rounds would ask the head nurse if she had given the children the bottle but asked no other questions. Nobody seemed to know exactly what went into the bottle, but Collins, blaming the surgeon, says, 'He knew well enough what the bottle was made up of, and that the children derived assistance from its contents. They were being assisted to die.'

Despite many futile attempts to reform the hospital, it was finally shut down in 1826. During the last thirty years of its sorry existence, of the 52,000 children admitted to the hospital, 41,500 died in its care.

Jack Langan

Jack Langan, the famous bare-knuckle boxer, was born in May 1798 at the beginning of the Rebellion. There has been some confusion as to his place of birth. His friend and biographer Pierce Egan claims in his *Boxiana, or Sketches of Pugilism*, that Jack was born at a place called Clondalton in County Kildare, but it seems likely that he was referring to Clondalkin in County Dublin, which was then a rural village.

Jack's family moved to Ballybough, close to the infamous Mud Island, where Jack's parents carried on a 'provisions business' when Jack was still a toddler. Mud Island was a no-go area where local lore had it that 'a bailiff has not showed his unlucky face, except at a wake, a christening or a wedding, and then only in the way of friendship.'

From a very young age Jack had developed 'a taste for milling', and his childhood days were filled with punch-ups. His first proper bare-knuckle bout is said to have taken place on the banks of the canal when he was thirteen: he took on and beat a youth who was five years older – and much bigger – than him.

After a short spell at sea Jack returned to Ballybough, where he found work at a local sawmill, and it wasn't long before he took up where he had left off on the pugilistic front. Langan quickly made a name for himself as a scrapper when he got involved in a row with two Mud Island hard men named Jemmy Lyons and Jack Reilly following a snowball-throwing incident.

Langan became a marked man after that and he was challenged by another islander, Pat MacGuire. Langan gave MacGuire such a hiding that he had to be carried home to his bed. He said afterwards that the punches Langan had given him were more like the kicks of a horse than the punches of a man. Langan was still only sixteen years old at that time.

In another canal-side fight between Langan and an opponent called Savage that is detailed in *Sketches of Pugilism*, Langan hit Savage so hard that it was feared he had killed him. The unfortunate Savage was carried home, where his corpse was washed and laid out for a wake. At some stage during the proceedings, the house was cleared very rapidly when the corpse sat up abruptly, demanding to know what had happened to him.

After spending some time in South America and the Caribbean, Jack again returned to Dublin, where he ran a pub in King Street for a time. The pub was called The Sign of the Irish Arms, and a plaque referring to Jack bore the legend: 'Quiet when Stroked, Fierce when Provoked'. Jack was later forced to flee to England following a fling with a young dairymaid named Cathy Flynn, who took a paternity suit against him and won damages of a hundred pounds.

The highlight of Langan's boxing career came when he twice fought Tom Spring, 'Champion of England and all the civilised world', in 1824. The first fight, which lasted a staggering seventy-seven rounds, took place at Worcester Racecourse on 7 January 1824 in front of a crowd of at least thirty thousand spectators. Spring was declared the winner after Langan was unable to come out for the seventy-eighth round. A rematch took place near Chichester in June that year: after another gruelling bout, lasting for seventy-six rounds this time, Spring again emerged as the victor. Although Jack was only twenty-six years old, he retired from the ring after the fights with Spring and became a publican in Liverpool. He made enough money from this venture to retire to Cheshire, where he died at the age of only forty-eight on St Patrick's Day 1846.

THE LOCK HOSPITAL

Way back in the early 1970s, I can remember the folk group Prosperous singing a ballad entitled 'The Lock Hospital'. The song relates the sad tale of a young VD-ridden squaddie who, on his deathbed, warns others to 'beware of the flash-girls that roam through the city, for the girls of the city were the ruin of me'.

The hospital referred to in the song was situated somewhere in England, but there was an Irish version of the Lock Hospital in Dublin. The Westmoreland Lock Hospital for Incurables – or, to give it its official name, the Hospital of St Margaret of Cortona – was situated on Townsend Street. The Lock was founded in 1792 and was one of the few establishments catering for venereal disease. Initially, the hospital treated three hundred patients of both sexes. Later, its capacity was reduced to a hundred and fifty beds, and only women were admitted. Catholics and Protestants were segregated, while married women who had been infected by their husbands were kept away from common prostitutes.

In 1794, the Lock Penitentiary opened for business. The penitentiary catered for women who had been discharged from the hospital. The women were, as Samuel Lewis put it in his *Topographical Dictionary* in 1837, 'employed in needlework and other female occupations'. The Lock – which was once described as a 'monument to moral degradation' – was more like a prison than a hospital. It was a dreary, monotonous and depressing place. Patients were made to wear drab clothing lest they offend the sensibilities of the governors of the hospital. Explaining this policy, a witness to a government commission on Dublin hospitals said, 'If we allowed these swell ladies from Mecklenburgh Street [Monto] to flit about in pink wrappers and so on, it would be a distinct inducement to others less hardened to persevere in that life [prostitution] in the hope that probably they would arrive at similar distinction.'

During the last two decades of the nineteenth century, venereal disease was rampant in the city and it was estimated that in 1880 over a third of the five-thousand-strong Dublin garrison of the British army was infected with it. In 1881 a British commander complained that half the unmarried men in his regiment had succumbed to the disease. The situation got so bad at one stage that it led one commentator to suggest that prostitutes were doing a better job of weakening Ireland's links with the British Empire than nationalists. Despite the obvious fact that prostitution was a huge industry in Dublin, the subject was rarely mentioned and the Lock was largely ignored by the public.

At that time, many of Dublin's hospitals were maintained by the myriad charities that were operating in the city. Because prostitution and venereal disease were such distasteful subjects, the Lock never received any charitable donations from these organisations. As a result, the hospital faced a constant struggle for survival. Its main source of income was from government grants: the British War Office contributed £1,100 for the years 1899 to 1906. There were few donations from the public. From 1901 to 1906, an average of seven pounds per year was raised, and from 1907 to 1913 the donations amounted to one pound per annum. The Lock was finally closed in the 1950s and the building was demolished.

FIRES AND FIRE ENGINES

During the Middle Ages in Dublin, fire was a much greater danger than it is today because many of the city's public buildings and dwelling houses were made of wood. Large areas of the city were burned down in fires in 1190, 1192 and 1283. In 1304, a devastating blaze destroyed a great part of St Mary's Abbey, and St Patrick's Cathedral was damaged by fire in 1362. Fires had become so prevalent by the beginning of the fourteenth century that the Common Council of Dublin, in an attempt to curb the problem, issued the following order concerning the starting of fires: 'For fire taking place in any house from which flames issue not, the house-holder, after the flame has been extinguished, is liable to a fine of twenty shillings. If the flames be visible externally, the fine is forty shillings. Any person answerable for the burning of a street shall be arrested, cast into the middle of the fire, or pay a fine of 100 shillings.' In 1546, the Common Council ordered that 'twelve grips of iron shall be made for pulling houses that shall chance to be afire'. They also ordered forty leather buckets for carrying water.

At the beginning of the eighteenth century, the Lord Mayor of Dublin appointed a committee to look after the city's fire-fighting requirements. The committee recommended that 'two water engines of the best sort' be provided, one to be purchased from London immediately and another to be made in Dublin. The committee also recommended the building of a house to store the engines in. Although no firemen were provided to work these engines, the Dublin police and parish beadles were expected to rush to the site of a fire and help in 'the extinguishing of the fire and causing people to work at the engines for throwing up the water'.

Two of these old manually operated water engines can still be seen in the porch of St Werburgh's Church. One of the pumps dates from the seventeenth century, while the larger one was used as the parish fire engine during the eighteenth and nineteenth centuries.

During the late seventeenth and early eighteenth centuries, most fire-fighting in the city was carried out by insurance companies, which suffered huge losses from fire. These companies extinguished fires only in the property of their own clients; they identified their subscribers by a distinctive fire-mark nailed up at the front of the property.

The Dublin Fire Brigade Act of 1862 was the first real attempt to provide an organised fire-fighting facility for the city. The first superintendent of the brigade was a Dublin man, J. R. Ingram. Ingram had worked as a volunteer fireman in New York and had also spent time with the London Fire Service. A fire station was established at the City Assembly House in South William Street. The new station, in the basement of the Assembly Rooms, housed nine men and contained one small engine. A sub-station, connected by telegraph to South William Street, was established in Whitehorse Yard, just off Winetavern Street. This station, which was manned by fifteen firemen, contained three fire engines and ten water carts. Seven mobile fire escapes were also placed at strategic locations throughout the city.

THE PITT STREET NUNNERY

The first edition of the memoirs of the notorious Dublin madam Peg Plunket was published under the title of *Memoirs of Mrs Margaret Leeson* in 1795. Not for a very long time had the publication of any biography caused such consternation and panic amongst the ranks of Dublin's ruling classes.

The celebrated Peg Plunket, also known as Margaret Leeson, was born into a wealthy Westmeath family in 1727. Her clients included a bishop, two lord lieutenants, a governor of the Bank of Ireland and the infamous 'Sham Squire', Francis Higgins.

Peg's first venture was a brothel in Drogheda Street (now O'Connell Street), which she ran in partnership with another famous madam, Sally Hayes. For a time, the madams, as Peg tells us, 'lived like princesses' at Drogheda Street. They had a box at the theatre and frequently travelled to the races at the Curragh in their coach. Their idyllic existence came to an end when they were forced to leave Drogheda Street after a 'brat pack' known as the 'Pinkindindies', led by the balloonist Richard Crosbie, wrecked the brothel during a riot.

Peg had Crosbie – whom she referred to in her memoirs as 'Mr Balloon' – arrested and prosecuted for the attack on her house. Crosbie threatened to kill her and he was sent to Newgate Prison for a spell. He was eventually released after Wolfe Tone interceded with Peg on his behalf; Tone told her that the authorities 'would surely hang him' if she proceeded with the case.

She then moved on to a premises at Wood Street; one of her regular visitors there was the Bank of Ireland Governor,

David La Touche (1729–1817), who, according to Peg, spent most of his time admiring himself in her large looking-glass.

In 1784 Peg opened a new high-class brothel in Pitt Street, on the site where the Westbury Hotel now stands. This establishment, which was sometimes known as 'the Pitt Street Nunnery', was staffed by liveried servants, footmen and a coach driver and, in Peg's own words, 'a fresh importation of delicious Filles-de-Joys', recruited from the brothels of Covent Garden and Drury Lane in London.

One of the first visitors to the new establishment was Charles Manners, Duke of Rutland and Lord Lieutenant of Ireland, who, to the amusement of the citizens gathered outside, emerged from the brothel after a period of sixteen hours. His troop of horse guards were not so amused, however, as they had had to wait outside for him throughout the cold November night. The duke obviously enjoyed his stay at Peg's, as he arranged for her to receive a pension of three hundred pounds a year under an assumed name.

Peg was also married for a very brief period to Barry Yelverton Junior, the profligate son of the Chief Baron of the Irish Exchequer. The Chief Baron gladly handed over five hundred guineas to Peg to have the marriage annulled.

Peg's career took a sudden dive in 1794 when she ran out of money and was arrested and locked up in a debtor's prison. She was released following the intervention of her friends, who combined to pay her debts, and she wrote her memoirs soon afterwards to raise some money. Peg suffered further misfortune when she was raped by five men on her way home from a friend's house in Drumcondra. She contracted venereal disease as a result of the attack and died at a friend's house in Fownes Street three months later, in March 1797. She was buried in St James's churchyard in James's Street and her obituary was carried in the *Dublin Evening Post* and the London-based *Gentleman's Magazine*.

ADVICE FROM THE STARS

One of the most notorious residents of Nicholas Street in Dublin during the seventeenth and early eighteenth centuries was the self-appointed Doctor John Whalley (1653–1724). Whalley – as can be seen in the verse below – began his career as a humble shoemaker and went on to become the city's best-known astrologer, fortune-teller, weather forecaster, quack, publisher and newspaper proprietor.

> Whalley bred up to end and awl
> to work in garret or in stall
> Who had more skill in cutting leather
> Than foretelling wind and weather
> Forsook the trade of mending shoes
> To deal in politics and news
> Commenced Astrologer and Quack
> To raise the devil in a crack
> Told fortunes and could cure all ills
> With his elixirs and his pills

Whalley was virulently anti-Catholic. In 1688 he was punished for his rantings against the Pope and placed in the stocks at the Tholsel, where he was pelted with rotten eggs and vegetables. During King James II's brief stay in Dublin, Whalley, fearing for his life, took refuge in England. Following James's flight from Dublin, Whalley was safe to return, and he set himself up at the 'Blew Posts' on Stephen's Green, where he produced his astrological charts and predictions in a pamphlet entitled *Advice from the Stars*. In 1698 he moved to a house next door to the Fleece Tavern on Nicholas Street, where he produced various works concerning astrology.

Ten years later Whalley had moved again and had established himself as a publisher at the 'Blew Ball' just outside St Nicholas's Gate. In 1714 he published a newspaper entitled *Whalley's Newsletter* which contained news from home and abroad.

Whalley died in 1724. The following verse – taken from an elegy written by Jonathan Swift – is generally believed to have been composed for Whalley, although one writer claims that it was actually written in honour of another Dublin 'quack' named Partridge who died sixteen years before Whalley.

> Here five foot deep lies on his back
> A cobbler, starmonger and Quack
> Who to the stars in pure good will
> Does his best to look upward still
> Weep all ye customers who use
> His pills, his almanacs and shoes

After Whalley's death, Isaac Butler of Bull Alley – a former pupil of Whalley's – took over his master's mantle as Dublin's number one astrologer. Astrology was an extremely competitive business in those days and the Dublin practitioners never passed up an opportunity to discredit their rivals in their various publications. Butler's main rival was an astrologist named La Boissière, and Butler set out to discredit him in his almanac *A Voice from the Stars*. He constructed a chart for La Boissière using his birth date and the positioning of the stars and planets and he confidently predicted that La Boissière would die on a certain day.

Unfortunately for Butler, La Boissière survived, but on the very day in question, Butler's own father was knocked down and killed by a horse and cart! You would imagine that would have been the end of the story but La Boissière – in the next issue of his own almanac – had the bad taste to ask Butler why he hadn't predicted his own father's death and kept him at home on the day of the accident.

Butler's own death notice, recorded in the minutes of a body called the Medico-Philosophical Society in 1755, makes interesting reading:

On Tuesday last, at seven minutes four seconds past three, Post Meridian descended to the Antipodes or Nadir at his lodgings under the sign of Leo in Taurus, or Bull Alley, Dublin the Umbra or Penumbra of Mr Isaac Butler, Ptolemean Philomath, Judicial Astrologer, Discoverer of Losses, Botanist and Calculator of Nativities . . . This truly great adept departed this life, having hastened his end, by laudanum taken in brandy, which he prescribed for himself, in order to die like Socrates and other ancient sages.

The Sham Squire

Somewhere within the walls of the old Kilbarrack graveyard just off the Howth Road lie the remains of Francis Higgins, who was better known by his nickname 'the Sham Squire'. He was born in a Dublin cellar in 1746 and rose, by various means, from the lowly position of messenger boy to the ownership of the *Freeman's Journal*.

His parents came from a poor background in County Down and his father found employment as a law clerk. Francis was sent to work at an early age, running errands and shining shoes in Fishamble Street. His first break came when he obtained employment in an attorney's office in St Patrick's Close. This gave him an opportunity to forge documents that portrayed him as a man of means with a large estate and an income of three thousands pounds a year.

The ambitious young Higgins began to seek out eligible young women who could provide him with money and a step up the social ladder. He found what he was looking for in Mary Anne Archer, daughter of a very wealthy and respectable Dublin merchant. He arranged a meeting with her father through a priest and passed himself off as the son of a gentleman and a nephew of a Member of Parliament. Archer was convinced that Higgins would be an excellent match for his daughter, even though Mary Anne found Higgins to be physically repulsive. The couple married and moved to Lucan. It didn't take long for Mary Anne to discover that her new husband was a penniless chancer, and she went back to her parents. Higgins followed her and tried to gain entry to the house. In the struggle that ensued, Mrs Archer's arm was broken. A court case followed and Higgins was imprisoned for a year for fraud. During the course of the trial, the judge referred to Higgins as a 'sham squire'. Mary Anne died soon afterwards.

On his release from prison, Higgins began to accumulate money by selling smuggled tea to Dublin merchants. He then passed on the merchants' names to the Revenue and collected the reward money for informing on them. Then he invested his ill-gotten gains in brothels and gambling dens. He was made president of the Guild of Hosiers in 1775 and, despite his earlier prison sentence, became an attorney-at-law.

Higgins was also a loan shark. On learning that the owner of the *Freeman's Journal* was in debt, he offered to loan him money. Higgins waited until the proprietor was in even deeper trouble, then suddenly called in the debt. Unable to pay and facing the prospect of a spell in jail, the unfortunate man was forced to give Higgins ownership of the newspaper. Higgins became a very wealthy man and moved into an extremely fashionable residence on Stephen's Green, where he lived the life to which he had always aspired.

Higgins died suddenly in January 1802 at the age of fifty-six. Uncharacteristically, he left the bulk of his fortune to several Dublin charities. He also made provision for a substantial tomb to be erected over him at Kilbarrack. He rested in peace for almost half a century, until a second-hand bookseller called Fitzpatrick managed to obtain some Dublin Castle secret-service notebooks. Fitzpatrick concluded that the 'F.H.' named in the books as having been paid a thousand pounds for passing on information as to the whereabouts of Lord Edward Fitzgerald was Francis Higgins, the 'Sham Squire'. On hearing this news, a band of Dublin men marched out to Kilbarrack and smashed the tomb to pieces with sledgehammers. There is no trace of the tomb left today.

THE THOLSEL

Jury's Inn, just across the road from Christchurch Cathedral at the junction of Nicholas Street and Christchurch Place, marks the site of the ancient Tholsel. The Tholsel was built in the early fourteenth century as a meeting place for the Lord Mayor and the citizens of Dublin.

The name 'Tholsel' means 'toll seat' or 'toll stall' and is derived from the place where market tolls or taxes were paid. The Tholsel functioned as Dublin's City Hall and had many uses: it was primarily a meeting place for the members of Dublin Corporation, but on occasion it also served as a courthouse and jail.

In 1328 it was recorded that the Wicklow outlaw David O'Toole, 'a stout marauder, an enemy to the king and a burner of churches', was captured and brought before two judges at the Tholsel, where he was sentenced to be 'drawn at the tails of horses through the middle of the city as far as the gallows, and afterwards hanged upon a gibbet.'

All kinds of public meetings were held at the Tholsel, and in 1590 Adam Loftus, Archbishop of Dublin, addressed the Lord Mayor and Corporation of Dublin there. He asked for their permission to use the old priory of All Hallows for the construction of a new university there. His request was granted and two years later he established Trinity College on the site.

By the middle of the seventeenth century, the building was beginning to show signs of wear and tear, and in 1683 it was demolished and a new enlarged and improved Tholsel was erected on the site. Like the old Tholsel, the new building had several functions. It housed a criminal court that tried all crimes except treason and murder, and a civil court that dealt with minor claims amounting to no more than forty shillings. In another part of the building, the mayor and aldermen of Dublin met to conduct the day-to-day business of the city.

Criminals convicted at the Tholsel could expect to be publicly whipped on the back of a cart all the way from there to Hoggen Green (College Green), where they were either put in the stocks or flogged at the city pillory. Public book-burnings also took place at the Tholsel, along with the burning of illegal gambling tables and counterfeit goods.

As well as the above, the Tholsel was a major venue for banquets and feasts laid on by the city fathers. At certain times of the year, the exterior of the building was lit with candles, and free beer was dispensed to the citizens, who gathered outside around large bonfires.

In 1691, the corporation held a feast there in honour of King William of Orange's officer, General Ginkel, after his victory at the siege of Limerick. The evening was rounded off with a grand ball and firework display. Later that year, following the Battle of the Boyne, the Catholic citizens of Dublin were obliged to decommission their weapons at the Tholsel.

At the end of the eighteenth century, the Tholsel, which had been built on boggy ground, began to subside. The business of the court was transferred to Green Street, while the corporation moved to the Assembly Rooms on William Street.

A small part of the Tholsel continued in use as a court of conscience until 1809, when it was finally demolished.

WOLVES AND SUFFRAGETTES

Several years ago, it was suggested (quite seriously) to me that the name of Blanchardstown was derived from the French balloonist and inventor of the parachute, Jean-Pierre Blanchard, who died in 1809. The teller of this unlikely tale was adamant that old Jean-Pierre had crash-landed in a field near the village, having crossed over from France in a balloon. Now, while I am personally in favour of the old adage of never letting the truth get in the way of a good story, you have to draw the line somewhere.

The origins of the name 'Blanchardstown' actually date back to the thirteenth century. The first sighting of the name was in the form of 'Villa Blanchard'. The Blanchards, who were of Norman origin, appear to have been connected to Hugh Tyrell, First Baron of Castleknock. Another family connected to Tyrell were the Abbots who settled on the land now known as Abbotstown.

During the fifteenth century, special permission had to be given by Parliament to strike out several false deeds that had been manufactured by a Blanchardstown forger named Philip Cowherd. Using a false name, he claimed ownership of various properties and sold them to unwary buyers who 'knew not the law, and from one day to another menaced the tenants and freeholders'.

In seventeenth-century Ireland, conditions had been very favourable for the continued existence of the wolf population. Although their numbers had been drastically reduced by the deforestation of the country, many wolves still prowled the outskirts of Dublin. The problem was so bad that in 1652 a public wolf-hunt was organised at Scaldwood in Blanchardstown. The government paid a bounty for the head of a wolf – as much as six pounds for the head of a wolf bitch.

A survey carried out a few years later reveals that Blanchardstown was quite small at that time. The survey lists the village as containing only 'two thatched houses, a barn and a little cottage'. The cottage also contained an orchard, a garden and a waste mill. Shortly afterwards, a civil survey showed that there were thirty-one persons of full age living in the area: five of English descent and twenty-six Irish. The principal resident of Blanchardstown at that time was Richard Berford, who died in 1662, leaving behind – amongst other possessions – his brewing pan to the locals in Ratoath.

During the mid-1830s, Samuel Lewis's *Topographical Dictionary of Ireland* describes Blanchardstown as having fifty-seven houses with 342 inhabitants. It also had at that time a police station, a court of petty sessions, a chapel and a nunnery. The nuns ran a school in which two hundred poor children were taught. There were two other schools near the canal. The boys school was maintained by a Mr Morgan, while a woman named Mercer paid for the upkeep of a school for fifty young girls. Nearby, at Abbotstown, a mixed school was maintained by the Hamilton family, with some of the children receiving free clothing.

The suffragettes were active in Blanchardstown during the early part of the last century. Local woman Catherine Duffy was arrested on 9 June 1912. Following a protest march led by Hannah Sheehy-Skeffington, Duffy was charged with breaking seventeen panes of glass with a hammer. She was unrepentant afterwards, saying, 'If we have to wear out every hammer in the country smashing every pane of glass in the country, we will get our votes.'

The Brighton of Ireland

The coastal town of Bray in County Wicklow has been referred to over the years as 'the Gateway to Wicklow'; more popularly, it was called 'the Brighton of Ireland' during the nineteenth century. The name of the town comes from the Irish word *'brí'* or *'bre'*, which means simply 'hill'. In the case of Bray, the town gets its name from the eight-hundred-foot-high Bray Head, which overshadows the town.

The origins of the town stretch back to the twelfth century: Strongbow granted lands belonging to the O'Tooles and the Norseman Thorkil to the Norman lord Walter de Riedleford in 1173. De Riedleford is credited with the building of the castle close to where Bray Bridge now stands.

Throughout the course of the last eight hundred years, hardly a town or village on the borders of the Pale escaped the attention of the Wicklow tribes, the O'Byrnes and the O'Tooles, and Bray is no exception. Bray seemed to be particularly vulnerable to attack from the Wicklow Mountains, and a state of war between the invader and the dispossessed continued for centuries.

In 1313, the O'Tooles and the O'Byrnes swept down from their mountain strongholds and burned Bray, Arklow and Newcastle. The following year, the constable of Bray, Sir Hugh de Lawless, said that the lands had been 'invaded, burned and totally devastated by the Irish of the mountains'.

In 1394, another member of the Lawless family, William, was slain in an encounter with the Irish. Eight years later, in

1402, there was a battle near Bray, during which five hundred Irish are said to have been killed. The spot where they were killed was known as 'Bloody Bank', subsequently changed to 'Sunny Bank'.

In 1429, a large army of English soldiers assembled at Bray with the intention of doing battle with the O'Byrnes and the O'Tooles. They were described as being well stocked, with enough provisions for a long campaign, and equipped with giant catapults for hurling stones at their enemies. The 'burners' must have prevailed in the end, however, because by 1615 the vicar of Bray was one Maurice Byrne, who gave the church service in Irish.

Two hundred years ago, before the esplanade was built, the seafront at Bray was practically unused. The sand-duned and shingled shoreline was described as being dotted with great holes and hollows where farmers had taken the sand away. In addition, there was a rough and broken raised pathway that led to Bray Head.

There were two residences on the seafront at that time; Weston St John Joyce described one of them, known locally as 'the rat hole'. This building was a filthy mud hut, occupied by an eccentric fisherman who took it upon himself to surround the hut with piles of manure, offal and any other types of rotting materials that he could lay his hands on.

The very factor that hindered the growth of Bray over the centuries – its close proximity to the Wicklow mountains – led to its expansion and prosperity in the eighteenth and nineteenth centuries. During that period, tourists flocked to Bray in such large numbers that it came to be known as 'the Brighton of Ireland'.

In 1854, when the Dublin-to-Kingstown railway line was extended to the town, Bray became established as a popular seaside resort. The promenade, laid out by William Dargan, was built a few years later and hotels and guesthouses sprang up all along the seafront. There was even a Turkish bathhouse in the town. At the height of its popularity, the resort attracted up to four thousand visitors per day.

Buck Whaley

Back in eighteenth-century Dublin, the nickname 'Buck' was in as common usage as, for example, 'Whacker' is today. The name was attached to such worthies as Buck Jones of Clonliffe Road, Buck Lawless, Buck Sheehy and Buck English.

But without a doubt, the grand-daddy of all the Bucks was Buck Thomas Whaley, who was born in Dublin on 15 December 1766. He was the eldest son of Richard Chapell Whaley, who was given the nickname 'Burn-Chapel' when he burned down a Catholic church while taking part in a priest-hunting expedition.

Burn-Chapel died when the young Buck was only four years old, and he left him an estate of £7,000 per year and a lump sum of £60,000. When Buck was sixteen years old, he was sent to France to further his education in the company of a tutor – and with an allowance of £900 per annum.

After gambling a large portion of his fortune in France, Buck was treated like the prodigal son on his return to Dublin. Despite a whirlwind round of drinking, gambling and orgies, he soon grew restless, and he accepted a bet for £15,000 with his friends that he would travel to Jerusalem and return to Dublin within two years. He set off on 20 September 1788 and, after many adventures in the Holy Land, arrived back in Dublin in June or July of the following year, having fulfilled all the conditions of the bet.

One popular legend that arose out of Whaley's trip to the Holy Land was that he had agreed, as part of the wager, to play a game of handball against the walls of Jerusalem, but he makes no reference to such an incident in his memoirs. He did go to some lengths to obtain proof of his visit to Jerusalem: his memoirs contain a copy of a signed certificate that he received from the Superior of Terra Sancta in Jerusalem on 5 March 1789:

> I, the undersigned Guardian of this Convent of St Mary, certify to all and singular who may read these presents that Messrs Thomas Whaley and Hugh Moore have, on two occasions, been present and resided in this City of Nazareth for the space of three days, in witness whereof.

Armed with this proof, he returned to Dublin, and his friends reluctantly handed over the stake money of £15,000. The whole venture had cost him £8,000, so he came out £7,000 ahead. As Buck said in his memoirs, it was 'the only instance in all my life before, in which any of my projects turned out to my advantage'.

Buck remained in Dublin for the next two years, drinking, gambling and generally living the high life, until his credit ran out. He then went to London for a few years, becoming involved in several dubious enterprises there.

He was returned as MP for Newcastle, County Down, for a time and also represented Enniscorthy. While MP for Enniscorthy, he accepted a bribe of £4,000 to vote for the Union; he subsequently accepted a similar sum to vote against it.

When Buck died on a visit to Cheshire in England on 2 November 1800, the newspapers of the day reported that he had died from a 'rheumatic fever'. It was also rumoured that he had been stabbed to death by a jealous mistress who discovered that he had been engaged in an affair with her sister.

He was buried at Knutsford in Cheshire and it was reported that just before he was placed in his coffin an Irish dancer named Robinson danced a hornpipe on the lid.

NELSON'S PILLAR

On 18 November 1805 the Corporation of Dublin met and passed a resolution congratulating King George III on his victory at the Battle of Trafalgar. The Corporation decided to honour the architect of that victory – Lord Horatio Nelson – with a suitable memorial. One member suggested an oil painting, while others wanted a more permanent memorial. They decided to hold a public meeting to discuss a suitable project. A meeting of the 'nobility, clergy, bankers, merchants and citizens of the city' was held and a committee was formed. It was decided to build a pillar with a statue of Nelson on top. The committee, which included Arthur Guinness, collected £1,000 immediately, and by 12 December the same year they had collected nearly £4,000 for the project.

The building of the Pillar began in 1808 after objections from Sackville Street residents, who felt that the monument would bring too many sightseers to the area. They argued that it would be better located on the quays, where it would be more appreciated by incoming sailors. Despite these objections, the foundation stone of the pillar was laid with great pomp and ceremony on 15 February 1808, and it was opened to the public on the anniversary of the Battle of Trafalgar on 21 October 1809. The outside of the pillar was constructed from Wicklow granite, while the interior was of black limestone. The total height of the pillar and statue was 134 feet and it had an interior staircase with 168 steps.

The pillar became the focus for many strange incidents over the years. On 4 June 1881 the *Freeman's Journal* carried the headline: 'EXCITING SCENE AT NELSON'S PILLAR'. The 'exciting scene' was the commotion caused by a fifteen-year-old Dublin newspaper boy named John Connolly. Connolly sneaked up to the top of the Pillar without paying the usual fee of sixpence. He wasn't spotted until he emerged at the top of the pillar and began to run around and around shouting. When a large crowd had gathered down below in Sackville Street, the youth climbed over the railings on to the outer ring of the monument and began to charge around, holding the railing with just one hand. He was eventually caught by the pillar attendant and was handed over to two policemen, who took him to the police station in Store Street. He was charged the next day with obstruction, but he escaped with a tongue-lashing and a caution from the magistrate. Another incident took place in 1897 when a deranged man attempted to climb the flagpole at the top of the Pillar. He then tried to jump off the Pillar but was saved at the last moment by a policeman.

Nelson's Pillar was finally destroyed in March 1966 when it was blown up by the IRA. In the attempt to clear away the remains, the Irish army managed to blow out half the windows in O'Connell Street. Nelson's head can now be viewed at the Civic Museum in South William Street. The Dubliners later commemorated Nelson's demise in a ballad that referred to him as the first Irish astronaut.

SMOCK ALLEY

Essex Street West in Dublin's Temple Bar was known throughout the seventeenth and eighteenth centuries as Smock Alley. There is no hard evidence relating to the origin of this name, but an eighteenth-century scribe says that it was connected with a local 'sink of sin' called 'Mother Bungy's House'. The writer relates that when a local man was found murdered in her 'bottomless pit of wickedness', Mother Bungy's house was demolished by her angry neighbours.

Smock Alley was clearly a place of ill repute during those times. In 1768, a serious riot was sparked off there by the stabbing of a butcher named Callan. A gang of the butcher's friends gathered at the alley to seek retribution, and in the ensuing riot, they tore down every house there that was suspected of harbouring the culprits. The riot, which raged for several days, was of such ferocity that the garrison at Dublin Castle was sent into the alley to keep the peace. Right up until the end of the eighteenth century, Smock Alley was notorious for its gambling dens. In 1790, a house frequented by a conman nicknamed 'Mendoza' was raided by the police. There they found a quantity of loaded dice in the basement along with the skeleton of one of Mendoza's victims.

In 1662, a Scotsman name John Ogilby opened what was to become Dublin's longest-running theatre in Smock Alley. Nothing is known about the early history of the theatre until 1691, when the overcrowded upper balcony collapsed during a performance, killing three people and injuring many more.

In 1745, Thomas Sheridan, father of the dramatist Richard Brinsley Sheridan, took over the management of the theatre. The first difficulty that Sheridan faced in his new role was how to control the unruly mobs that filled the cheap seats of the upper gallery. The Dublin mob had taken to shouting at the musicians for their favourite tunes. When they didn't get their way, they would throw apples and oranges at the musicians. Later, they graduated to hurling stones and bottles at the orchestra, injuring them and breaking their instruments. The situation became so bad that the musicians were forced to perform behind the backdrop to the stage. In addition to these problems, Sheridan also had to deal with a bear-baiting pit in one part of the theatre and a brothel in another!

The theatre was the scene of many serious riots over the years. In January 1747, a young Galway man called Kelly caused mayhem in the theatre while 'inflamed with wine'. He climbed over the spikes at the front of the stage and attempted to indecently assault one of the actresses. Kelly was eventually subdued and ejected from the theatre, but he returned shortly afterwards with his friends and wrecked the stage and the green room backstage.

In 1779, a visitor to Dublin described Smock Alley as 'one of the most elegant and best constructed theatres in the three kingdoms.' Despite its elegance, however, the theatre was in financial trouble. Audience numbers had dwindled and the manager was unable to pay the actors and musicians. During a production of *Othello* in the late 1780s, the theatre manager was forced to play one of the leading roles. To add to his difficulties, he was forced to play the fiddle during the interval because the musicians had gone on strike. Smock Alley theatre finally closed its doors in 1790, after 128 years of productions.

Captain Dempsey

Down through the centuries, Dublin has had its fair share of eccentrics and characters, such as 'Bang-Bang', 'Forty-Coats', 'Zozimus' and 'Billy-in-the Bowl', to name but a few. But one of these 'knights of the road', called Captain Dempsey, has received scant attention over the years.

The eccentric figure of Captain Robert Dempsey was a familiar site on the streets of late-eighteenth-century Dublin as he went on his daily rounds through the city. The captain's favourite haunts were the lanes and alleyways in the vicinity of St Patrick's Cathedral.

Captain Dempsey was described as being a tall, lean man, with sunken eyes and a look of resignation on his face, 'over whose chin no razor had passed for years'. On his travels, he usually wore a long plaid shawl draped around his narrow shoulders, and a broad-brimmed hat. He wore breeches with leather patches sewed to the knees, and large silver buckles adorned his shoes.

The captain also wore several rings on his fingers; these rings seemed to be of great significance to him, as he would often stop suddenly in the street and stare intently at them, muttering to himself. He would then drop to his knees – ignoring the crowds of curious onlookers – and take off the rings, praying to each one in turn before carrying on with his journey, as if this was a perfectly normal thing to do.

Dempsey, a former seafarer and adventurer, lived in a ramshackle wooden hut on waste ground at the end of Townsend Street, overlooking the River Liffey and Dublin

Bay. Entrance to the hut was gained through a doorway in the roof, which could only be reached by a wooden ladder. There was a small window on the river side of the hut, and the captain would sit there for hours on end gazing out at the river and the sea beyond.

The captain was particularly renowned for his mercurial mood swings. On his good days, he would sit outside his little hut chatting easily with the inhabitants of Townsend Street but then suddenly, without warning, he would run into the hut and slam the door in the face of the person he had just been talking to. He would then retreat into a cellar he had dug underneath the hut; the cellar contained a small altar lit by two oil lamps.

He would often remain in the cellar for days on end, until his anger had subsided. His neighbours were well used to these tantrums, and when he re-emerged, they would bring him food and drink, as he wouldn't take any sustenance during his periods of self-enforced confinement. He had a particular liking for herrings, which were at that time to be found in great abundance in the shallow waters of Dublin Bay, and he was rarely seen without a few of them hanging from his cloak.

Captain Dempsey died in 1802 and his body lay undiscovered for a whole week. It was believed that he died from a seizure. Visitors to his hut discovered his lifeless body beside the little altar that he had built underground.

ISOLDE'S CHAPEL

The village of Chapelizod near Palmerstown wasn't named after a long, green, scaly creature, as one English scribe must have supposed in a seventeenth-century survey when he described the village as 'Chapel Lizard'.

The name is derived from the Irish '*Séipéal Isolde*', meaning Isolde's Chapel. Isolde is believed to have been the daughter of a sixth-century Irish king called Angus. The original site of Isolde's Chapel is thought to be the current site of the Church of Ireland.

There was at one stage in the village of Chapelizod a large building known as the 'Brass Castle'. Very little has been written about the history of the building, but J. S. Le Fanu's novel *House by the Churchyard*, set in Chapelizod, mentions the Brass Castle as being the residence of the villain of the piece.

There was a hospital for the treatment of lepers in the townland of St Laurence between Chapelizod and Palmerstown. The disease must have been quite prevalent in the city during the Middle Ages because this was one of two leper hospitals in Dublin.

The other one, the Leper Hospital of St Stephen, was on the spot of the old Mercer's Hospital near Stephen's Green. The owners of the hospital also had lands at Leopardstown in south Dublin. The area was called Lepers Town until the eighteenth century. Perhaps the name-change was instigated by eighteenth-century land speculators who realised that the association with leprosy wouldn't do much for house prices in the area!

In the eighteenth century, Chapelizod became a popular residential suburb, located as it is just four miles from the city centre. Among the local homeowners were retired army officers, wealthy Dublin merchants and doctors. In 1747, the Lord Mayor of Dublin, Richard White, lived in Chapelizod.

In that era, Chapelizod was also famous as a place of entertainment, with many taverns. To this day, the Mullingar House pub in Chapelizod recalls a link to the time when a stagecoach for Mullingar passed through Chapelizod and Palmerstown. The Mullingar House features prominently in James Joyce's *Finnegans Wake*.

The era of modern transport is also associated with Chapelizod: the first steam train was put on the road on 2 June 1881 by the Dublin–Lucan Steam Train Company, and for the first few months it ran only as far as Chapelizod. As we face disruption in Dublin for the creation of the LUAS line, it is interesting to note that the completion of the train line to Lucan was delayed for two years due to unrest in the country.

At first there were three classes of travel on the line, but second-class travel was later eliminated. The third-class fare to Riverside, Chapelizod, was one penny. In 1900, the company electrified the line and changed its name to 'the Dublin to Lucan Electric Railway Company'.

Towards the end of the last century, clay-pigeon shooting was very popular in Dublin and the gentry flocked to Chapelizod in elegant horses and carriages to indulge in the sport in the gently rolling pastures. Duck shooting was also popular, and brought much business to the local hostelries as the gentry disported themselves with refreshments at the end of the day.

'The Most Charitable City in the World'

The poverty-stricken and slum-ridden Dublin of the eighteenth and nineteenth centuries has often been described as 'the most charitable city in the world'. There were a large number of benevolent institutions within the city at that period; many of these institutions are listed in J. J. McGregor's *Picture of Dublin*, published in 1821, and Whitelaw, Warburton and Walsh's *History of Dublin*, published three years earlier.

One of these was St James's Widows House in James's Street also has an interesting history. This charity was founded by a humble jarvey named John Loggins in 1771. Loggins, from Bow Bridge, was an industrious man and through his own efforts he managed to save enough money to buy two coaches. He soon built up a lucrative business driving judges around the country when they went on circuit, and soon enough Loggins had enough money to invest in a large house at Bow Bridge.

Loggins had, however, one flaw in his character that nearly led to his downfall – a love of drink. He would get so drunk on occasion that he would have to be carried home in a basket on the back of a porter. He made several attempts to give up drinking, but finally succeeded after a drunken incident in which he was nearly killed by a horse. He then gave up the gargle for good and, like Matt Talbot in later years, turned to religion in gratitude for what he considered to be divine deliverance. He sold his coaches and horses and fasted and prayed for two days each week.

At the same time, Loggins single-handedly converted the stables at his house at Bow Bridge into a refuge or almshouse for destitute widows. Initially, he was able to provide shelter for six widows but by the time of his death in 1774 he had added enough rooms to cater for twenty.

After Loggins's death, the upkeep of the almshouse passed to the vicar of St James's parish, and early in the nineteenth century the widows were receiving three shillings and threepence per week, half a loaf and a clothing allowance, we are told by Whitelaw, Warburton and Walsh.

TIGER ROCHE

Sir Boyle Roche (1743–1807), who lived and died at 63 Eccles Street, served as an officer with the British army in America for seven years. On his return to Ireland, he entered parliament, and represented various boroughs until the Act of Union was passed in 1801. He was totally opposed to Catholic emancipation and was a staunch supporter of the British government. As a reward for his loyalty, he was made chamberlain to the viceregal court and was created a baronet in 1782. Roche was guilty of a few Dan Quayle-isms in his day. The most famous of these was: 'Why should we do anything for posterity? What has posterity ever done for us?' He once said during a debate that his love for Ireland and England was so strong that he 'would have the two sisters embrace like one brother'. Another gem was: 'No man can be in two places at once, like a bird.' Once he was worried that the French would invade Ireland and he warned in parliament that they would 'break in, cut us to mincemeat and throw our bleeding heads upon that table, to stare us in the face.'

Sir Boyle's brother, Tiger Roche (born 1729), was a Dublin 'rake' who was known in equal measures for his fondness for duelling and his love of drink. At the age of sixteen he came to the attention of the viceroy, Lord Chesterfield, who offered him a commission in the army. Tiger had other ideas, however, and sought the company of like-minded young rakes. He was forced to flee Ireland after killing a nightwatchman during a drunken brawl. Roche managed to escape to Cork and from there he boarded a ship bound for North America.

On reaching that country, he joined the French army and fought with them against the native American Indians. When England and France declared war on each other; Tiger went over to the English side and became an officer. His career in the English army ended when he was accused of stealing a gun from a fellow officer and was court-martialled. He was dismissed from the army 'with ignominy'. Tiger hotly disputed the judgement against him and challenged his accuser to a duel, which the officer hastily declined. In a rage he attacked his guard. Before anyone could stop him, he had sunk his teeth into his accuser's throat and torn away a large mouthful of flesh. He often said afterwards that it was 'the sweetest morsel I have ever touched'. It was from this incident that he earned the nickname 'Tiger'. Shortly afterwards, a corporal named Burke confessed on his deathbed that he had committed the offence, and Roche was reprieved and given a new commission. He returned to Dublin, where he received a hero's welcome. News of his exploits had spread far and wide and he was fêted wherever he went.

Tiger Roche went to live in London, where he fell on hard times. He swindled two young women out of their fortunes and spent some time in a debtors' prison as a result. Roche then decided to try his luck in India, but he was arrested and tried in Cape Town for the murder of a Captain Ferguson following a row during the voyage. He was acquitted and sent back to London. He was tried for the same murder at the Old Bailey in 1775 and was again acquitted. The next year he went to India and was never heard from again.

The Bathing Island

One hundred years ago, it was still possible at low tide to see the remnants of Clontarf Island, which was located about 150 metres out from where the East Wall Road now runs. This island, 500 metres long by 100 metres wide, was, until the nineteenth century, a prominent Dublin landmark. It had at one time been much further out in the bay, but the combined effects of silting and extensive land-filling along the old shoreline at North Strand, Fairview and the North Wall eventually brought the city to within spitting distance of the island.

One of the first mentions of the island was in 1538, when a lease for it and the rest of Clontarf was granted to the King family by the prior of Kilmainham. The Kings had extensive fishing interests in Dublin Bay and they held the island until 1640, when they were dispossessed by the Cromwellians. There are conflicting accounts as to who got their hands on the island next. One report states that it was given to John Blackwell, a close ally of Cromwell, while others suggest that it was granted to a Captain Cromwell, a relative of Oliver.

During the 1660s, the government was concerned about the effects of a plague sweeping through the streets of London and adopted contingency plans in case the disease appeared in Dublin. The Lord Deputy ordered that two houses be built on Clontarf Island for the reception and control of any would-be carriers of the disease.

Throughout the eighteenth century, the island, then known as 'the bathing island', became a popular place to go at weekends. During the summer months, boatloads of Dubliners were transported from the wharf at East Wall to swim at the 'bathing pond' on the island. This was apparently a safe swimming area where, Dillon Cosgrave says, 'swimming with corks was practised'.

Nineteenth-century Dubliners knew the island as 'Cromwell's Island', after Christopher Cromwell, a Dublin publican who occupied it for a time. Cromwell built a wooden house on the island and often stayed there, spending lazy days swimming and fishing with his family.

Cromwell's peaceful idyll was shattered on the night of 9 October 1844 during one of the worst storms ever recorded in Dublin Bay. There was extensive flooding in Dublin that night and at the East Wall it was so severe that waves were reported to have washed over the roof of the Wharf Tavern.

Cromwell's house was swept away during the storm, and the next morning the bodies of Cromwell and his ten-year-old son William were discovered on the shore of the island. The remnants of their little wooden house, which had been carried away by the storm, were discovered against the embankment of the Great Northern Railway line at the present-day junction of the Howth and Malahide Roads, while their boats were found at Annesley Bridge.

Today, no trace remains of Clontarf Island. Over the course of the eighteenth and nineteenth centuries, the island got smaller and smaller as a result of it being used as a quarry in the construction of the South Wall and the North Lotts. The island finally disappeared during the latter part of the nineteenth century, when vast quantities of shelly sand were removed from the island to be used as fertiliser.

THE STREET OF THE COOKS

Cook Street, just off Winetavern Street, is one of the oldest streets in Dublin and has been in existence since the fourteenth century. In his *History of the City of Dublin*, John Gilbert says that the street was originally known as 'Vicus Cocorum', meaning 'the Street of the Cooks'. It was also described in early records as 'Le Coke Street'. As the name implies, the street was originally inhabited by the cooks of Dublin and was full of their stalls and shops.

Cook Street was actually outside the walls of the old city. It has been suggested that this came about because of the unhygienic conditions that then existed within the confines of the city walls. At that time, Dublin streets would have been open sewers, with pigs running about freely.

The Anglo-Norman De Burnell family were among the first residents of Cook Street. The De Burnells were active in politics, and in 1535 one of their number, John Burnell, was executed at Tyburn for his part in the revolt of 'Silken Thomas' Fitzgerald. Another family member, Henry Burnell, was placed under house arrest in 1605 for making representations to the government on behalf of Dublin's Catholics.

In 1623, another Cook Street resident, a former Lord Mayor of Dublin, Sir James Carroll, was accused of giving shelter at his home to 'Jesuits, friers and popish priests. On 23 January of that year, the Council of Ireland issued a proclamation ordering the banishment of the same 'Jesuits, friers and popish priests' out of Ireland within forty days. For many years, Cook Street was a refuge for the priests, monks and nuns of the Franciscan, Dominican and Carmelite orders.

On St Stephen's Day, 1629, a band of musketeers led by the Protestant Archbishop of Dublin, Dr Launcelot Bulkeley, destroyed the Franciscan monastery in Cook Street. The musketeers tore down the chapel, dispersing the Mass-goers in the process, and pulled down a statue of St Francis. A mob of angry Catholics soon gathered, and the archbishop was forced to hide in a nearby house.

As a result of this incident, King Charles I decreed that the house be demolished, and all Franciscan schools throughout the country were dissolved. It is not clear whether the order was carried out, however, as the Franciscans were back in business in Cook Street less than twelve months later.

During the mid-nineteenth century, a Dublin publisher named John Nugent printed *Old Moore's Almanac* in Cook Street. One of Nugent's rivals referred to the almanac as 'the Rushlight of Coffin Colony'. This was a reference to the fact that Cook Street was then the home of the coffin-makers of Dublin. During the early 1800s there were up to sixteen coffin-makers plying their trade in Cook Street, but by the end of that century there were only five.

CRY HELP IN COOLOCK

The name 'Coolock' comes from the Irish *'an Chúlóg'*, which means 'the Little Corner'. Over the centuries, it has been referred to as 'Culog', 'Culoc' and 'Cowlocke'.

During the 1830s, a writer made reference to the many ancient burial mounds discovered over the years at Coolock. One of these mounds is still in existence in the grounds of the Cadbury's chocolate factory, which was formerly known as Moatfield House – home of the famous novelist Charles Lever.

There were other burial mounds discovered in the area at Bonnybrook and Darndale, and close to the church at Edenmore. The Bonnybrook mound, close to Coláiste Dhúlaigh, was excavated during the 1930s. A farmer was ploughing a field near Bonnybrook House when he came across human remains. Newspapers of the day reported that something between ten and twenty skeletons were uncovered at the site. The National Museum thought that the site had been the scene of a battle sometime between the thirteenth and fifteenth centuries, while others put forward the argument that it had been a plague grave. In his excellent historical account of Coolock, *Green Fields Gone Forever*, Douglas Appleyard says that this field was known locally as the 'Cry Help' field. Apparently, survivors from the Battle of Clontarf (the author doesn't say from which side) were captured and slaughtered there in 1014.

During the early part of the Norman era, the De Nugent family were lords of Coolock. Gilbert de Nugent was given the lands at Coolock by Hugh de Lacey, Lord of Meath. One of the earliest references to the de Laceys' reign was a court case in 1207 involving the deceased Gilbert de Nugent and his brother Hacket.

One hundred years later, there was a reference to the death of Peter de Coulock, who died leaving thirty acres of land in the parish to his son Nicholas. This family was involved in the legal profession over several generations and their name appears frequently in the history of the area.

In 1836, Samuel Lewis tells us that the parish of Coolock contained 914 dwellers, with 190 of them inhabiting the village, which contained twenty-six houses and a police station. The area was known for its abundance of limestone quarries and for its beautiful (and then unhindered) views of Dublin Bay. Lewis also mentions that there was a great assembly at the commons near St John's Church in 1803 during the time of Robert Emmet's insurrection. Men from all over north Dublin and County Meath had gathered there to await a signal to march on Dublin, but the signal never came.

In 1832, a few years before Lewis was writing, Michael Staunton, proprietor of the *Morning Register* and *Evening Herald* newspapers, lived at Moatfield House. Staunton was concerned that too many of the agricultural labourers living in Coolock were spending their wages at the local taverns, so he set up a benefit scheme that would help them put their hard-earned money to good use.

His scheme was similar to today's system of credit unions. Members paid one shilling per week to the society but were not entitled to benefits until they had accumulated one pound. Only 'honest characters' were admitted to the scheme, and any member whose 'viciousness had been marked by conviction in a court of justice' was thrown out of the society.

Sick members of the society were entitled to seven shillings weekly, while the unemployed received five shillings a week.

Members were given £5 death benefit and also had their funeral expenses paid. The scheme thrived over the years, to such an extent that the society was able to offer loans to its members at a reasonable rate. During the 1830s, the society had an estimated membership of 300 people, the majority of whom were agricultural labourers.

CRIME AND PUNISHMENT

One of the most important trading areas in medieval Dublin was the Cornmarket, situated at the west end of High Street; many of the city's merchant classes lived in its immediate vicinity. A well-known feature of the Cornmarket at that time was the 'Bull Ring'. This was simply a large iron ring to which bulls were tied during the then-popular pastime of bull-baiting. It was customary during those times to elect a 'Mayor of the Bull Ring'. One of the mayor's duties was to ensure that the young people of the locality were in a state of constant readiness for battle and to provide soldiers for the mayor and sheriffs of Dublin during times of strife.

The Mayor of the Bull Ring was also responsible for the moral conduct of the bachelors of the area. When any of these young men got married, they were escorted from the church to the bullring by the mayor, where they were forced to pay homage to the ring with a goodbye kiss.

Keyzar's Lane in Cornmarket, described as a steep and slippery hill leading to Cook Street, was irreverently christened 'Kiss Arse' Lane by the locals. A Lord Mayor of Dublin, Jenico Marks, was killed in this lane during a riot in 1496.

The Cornmarket was one of the many sites in Dublin where public punishments were carried out throughout the Middle Ages. At one end of the market stood Newgate Prison, which was used as the city jail from the end of the fifteenth century. A gallows was erected there during the sixteenth century, and a priest named Michael Fitzsimons was hanged there in 1583.

As well as the routine hangings, floggings and burnings administered during those times, the city fathers managed to come up with some fairly innovative punishments involving public humiliation, as can be seen in a number of cases recorded by John Gilbert. In 1665, the Provost-Marshal of Dublin, Laurence Lambert, was found guilty of assaulting a member of the House of Commons. For his punishment, he was forced to stand 'without hat or cloak' at the Cornmarket scaffold and publicly confess his offence on the next market day.

Thirteen years earlier, a soldier named John Bayden was court-martialled for dereliction of duty. He was found guilty of the crime and for his sins he was ordered to 'ride the wooden horse for the space of an hour' at the Cornmarket. He was also forced to carry the wooden horse from the guardhouse to his place of punishment.

During the same year, an employee at Dublin Castle called Mabel Archbold was found guilty of spying and sentenced to be hanged at the Cornmarket. The court also decreed that all of her possessions and those of her husband be given to the informer who had given evidence against her.

One of the most novel forms of punishment inflicted at the Cornmarket was that administered to Connell Molloy, who had been convicted of forgery. The unfortunate Molloy was sentenced to stand in the pillory for three market days wearing a sign giving details of his crime, with his ears nailed to the pillory!

CRUMLIN RACES

The present district of Crumlin takes its name from the old Irish 'Croimmlinn', which translates as 'the crooked (or curved) valley'. In medieval times, Crumlin was one of the four royal manors of the English Crown. The others were Esker, Newcastle Lyons and Saggart.

During the sixteenth century, the residents of Crumlin were forced to pay a higher rent than the other manors because they had murdered the king's seneschal. The seneschal had abused the tenants during a court hearing and they turned on him and 'knocked their seneschal on the costard and left him there sprawling on the ground for dead'.

Like many other settlements on the borders of the Pale, Crumlin was vulnerable to attack from the dispossessed Irish in the Dublin and Wicklow Mountains. In 1331, three of the leading Normans of the district were killed by the O'Tooles in an ambush at a place called Culiagh near Crumlin.

In 1467, a resident petitioned the king for help. He had been taken hostage by the O'Tooles and was released only after paying a large ransom, which made him destitute. He also spoke of his great difficulty in finding tenants because of their fear of the rebels living in the nearby mountains.

In 1595, Crumlin was attacked and burned to the ground by Walter Reagh Fitzgerald and some of the sons of the famous Wicklow chief Fiach McHugh O'Byrne. During the course of the raid, the assailants stripped the lead roof off the local church to use the metal in the manufacture of bullets. It took the inhabitants a long time to recover from that particular attack. Twenty years later, the church had still not been repaired and the residents were said to be in a state of extreme poverty.

William of Orange camped at Crumlin for two days after the Battle of the Boyne in 1690. It was at Crumlin that he issued an edict banning King James II's famous 'brass money'.

The Court Book of Crumlin gives us some interesting insights into the everyday life of the inhabitants of the area in the sixteenth century. One case, in 1592, reveals that 'Patrick the swineherd' was charged with the theft of four sheaves of corn from his neighbour, Murrough Moore. During the same year, Patrick Brown and Allison White were fined for 'affray, assault and bloodshed' against Margaret Beaghan. The same court also ordered John Hoyles, the husband of Allison White, to clean up the mess made by his pigs on Crumlin common.

Horse racing was a popular pastime on Crumlin common but it was a great nuisance to the locals, who tried to disrupt the races in 1789. Backed up by the local magistrate and a strong force of soldiers, they attempted to move the race-goers on and tear down their tents and stalls. The race-goers ignored these attempts, however, and carried on with their racing, which lasted for several days.

With the beginning of the clearance of the slums of inner-city Dublin in the 1930s, the village of Crumlin was to change beyond all recognition. Nearly three thousand houses were built by Dublin Corporation in an attempt to alleviate the city's chronic housing problems. In 1936, the *Irish Press* described Crumlin as an idyllic, almost Utopian alternative to the crumbling tenements of the inner city:

Up here, in this airy, windswept, sun-bathed plateau, far from the squalor that palled their earlier times, there is being written for those reprieved slum denizens a chapter in what might well be titled "Paradise Regained". Here are flowers instead of cluttered garbage and debris; songbirds instead of the stifling effluvium of open drains; the rumbustious laughter of happy, healthy children instead of the querulous moaning of ailing little ones; hope instead of despair.

The King of Dalkey

The small island of Dalkey is separated from the shore of the mainland by a narrow stretch of water called the Dalkey Sound. The old Irish name for the island was 'Deilg Inis', meaning 'Thorny Island', and the name 'Dalkey' appears to be a Scandinavian version of the Irish name.

The island appears to have been inhabited from about 3000 BC, and a significant amount of Bronze Age beaker pottery was discovered there. The remains of a small promontory fort were also uncovered. The remarkably well-preserved remains of the church dedicated to St Begnet on the island date back to the eighth or ninth century.

There were several freshwater wells on the island; one of these – 'the scurvy well' – was believed to cure scurvy and many other diseases. There was also a 'fertile salt marsh' on Dalkey Island where sick cattle were taken to be cured and fattened. The island was used as a refuge in 1575 when it was recorded that many citizens of Dublin sought sanctuary there during an outbreak of plague in the city.

There are several smaller islands in close proximity to Dalkey Island. These are Lamb Island, Clare Rock and Maiden Rock. Tradition has it that Maiden Rock was so called because two maidens who had gone to the island to gather seaweed perished there during a sudden storm.

To the north of these small islands is a large group of rocks called the Muglins. In 1776, the bodies of two pirates who had been hanged for the murder of some of the crew of the *Sandwith* were hung up in irons from a gibbet erected at the Muglins as a warning to other wrongdoers. The bodies of the pirates, named McKinlie and Gidley, had previously been on display at Ringsend with those of two other pirates, but the bodies were removed, as they had proved to be 'very disagreeable to the citizens who walk there for amusement and health.'

For several years during the latter part of the eighteenth century, Dalkey Island annually played host to a very curious spectacle. The 'King of Dalkey' was the president of a satirical society formed in Fownes Street in Dublin sometime in the 1780s. Each year, the coronation of the president of the society, known as 'His Facetious Majesty, King of Dalkey, Emperor of the Muglins, Prince of the Island of Magee and Elector of Lambay and Ireland's Eye, Defender of His Own Faith and Respecter of All Others, and Sovereign of the Most Illustrious Order of the Lobster and Periwinkle' took place on the island.

The crowning of the last King of Dalkey, Stephen Armitage, occurred in 1797; the society was disbanded shortly afterwards due to the events of 1798. The society was described by one writer as 'the parent of secret democratic societies, in connection with the French revolutionists'.

The last 'coronation' at Dalkey is said to have attracted over twenty thousand spectators. The event was described by one newspaper as a 'glorious day' for the 'generous' Dalkey boatmen, who very obligingly rowed revellers out to the island for nothing but charged them a fortune to get back!

DONNYBROOK FAIR

The Middle Ages were a great era for fairs throughout Europe. The most important of these were the fairs at Champagne in France, Frankfurt and Leipzig in Germany and Milan in Italy, and there were also major fairs held at London and Stourbridge in England.

Some were set up for the sale of cattle, horses or agricultural produce, while others sold more general produce. Many trade fairs held pleasure or amusement fairs in conjunction with the main event. Over the years, some of the fairs lost their commercial focus and became purely pleasure fairs.

For over 600 years, the most important fair in this country was the Donnybrook Fair. It was first held in 1204, when King John granted a licence for the holding of an eight-day fair at Donnybrook. In 1215, he extended the fair to fifteen days and ordered that the first two days' revenue be given to the Archbishop of Dublin. The fair originally began on the feast day of the Invention of the Holy Cross – 3 May – but this was later changed to 21 March and finally to 26 August.

The Donnybrook Fair was held annually on a site where the Bective Rangers rugby club now stands. It took place in two fields, the larger of which was described as being crowded with horse-drawn caravans, mobile theatres and merry-go-rounds and a large number of booths and tents. One of the sideshows advertised in 1823 was Browne's Circus, whose main attraction was a handless Italian dwarf who specialised in 'sleight-of-hand and palmistry.' Also on show was a Russian dwarf and a dance involving nearly-naked 'savages'. The smaller field contained refreshment tents, which offered revellers beef, veal, chicken, ham, potatoes and 'gallons of punch'.

Like some of the European fairs, Donnybrook started out solely as a market for cattle and other produce. Over the years, the trade aspect of the fair diminished and the pursuit of pleasure and amusement took over. Although trading was still carried on – the horse trade was said to rival that of Ballinasloe – excessive drinking and violence became the fair's main focus. Today, many people – particularly Americans – associate the name of 'Donnybrook' with a row or riot.

As the years wore on, rioting became an annual feature of the fair; it was suppressed on several occasions as a consequence. In 1729, the fair was cancelled by the Lord Mayor of Dublin, while in 1751 Mayor Taylor ordered the sheriff to pull down all the tents and booths. The sheriff was forced to act later in the week when the Ormond and Liberty boys squared up to each other at the fair.

Donnybrook had acquired a bad reputation as a result of the fair, and in the 1830s some of the leading citizens began moves to have it closed down. One clergyman described it as 'a wild and reckless gathering of a multitude, devoted to all manner of unrighteousness'.

Reverend P. J. Nowlan of Donnybrook was the leading light in the campaign to have the fair suppressed. Along with other concerned citizens, he raised £3,000 to buy out the patent for the fair from the Madden family. The last fair was held in 1854.

God's Little Acre

In the November 1860 issue of the *Dublin Builder*, in an article entitled 'Saunterings in the Suburbs', the writer describes a trip to what was then the northside suburb of Drumcondra. He describes a visit to 'the fragment of a venerable elm popularly known as the Big Tree.' According to the unnamed scribe, the 'Big Tree' was the site of a well-known unofficial court of justice which was held in the immediate vicinity; a summons to the tree was regarded with the same seriousness as a visit to any formal court of law.

Legend has it that the tree was planted by Jonathan Swift. The elm, which was of enormous proportions, survived until 'the Night of the Big Wind' in 1839, when it was cut in half by the hurricane, after which there was 'nought but a wreck left behind.' The Big Tree Tavern in Dorset Street takes its name from these events; there has been an inn or tavern on this site for over five hundred years.

Also mentioned in the *Dublin Builder* was Jones's Road, which was originally built by Frederick 'Buck' Jones as a short cut to his home at the Red House, which is now the site of Clonliffe College. Jones didn't want to use Fortick's Lane (now Clonliffe Road) because it was a favourite haunt of footpads and highwaymen. Fortick's Lane was named after Tristram Fortick, who was previously owner of Clonliffe House. Fortick was the founder of a soup kitchen in Little Denmark Street.

Clonturk House in Drumcondra was once home to Duval, the famous dancing master. Duval discovered a spa well in the grounds of the house and decided to establish a sanatorium there for the exploitation of 'hypochondriacs and dyspeptics'. He also attempted to turn the estate and grounds into a pleasure garden modelled on the famous Vauxhall Gardens in London; he set up various types of amusements, including swings, hobby-horses and firework displays.

Close by, in Church Avenue, is Drumcondra churchyard, which is also known as 'God's Little Acre'. Some of the luminaries buried there include the architect James Gandon; Dr Benjamin Lentaigne, who treated Wolfe Tone on his deathbed; and Thomas Furlong, the Wexford poet. Another famous resident of the burial ground was Marmaduke Coghill, former MP and Chancellor of the Exchequer, who died in 1739. Coghill died a bachelor, probably on account of his often-expressed opinion that 'a man is entitled to beat his wife in moderation'!

A later headstone bears an inscription in memory of the 'Rajah of Frongoch'. Jimmy Mulkerns, who died in 1956, had been imprisoned at Frongoch internment camp in Wales after the 1916 Rising. During his time there, he often amused his fellow internees by dressing up as a rajah.

The *Dublin Builder* mentions a famous tavern opposite the graveyard that traded until around 1830. The name of the tavern is not given in the article but it was renowned for its food and was often used by Dublin Corporation for public dinners. The proprietor must have fallen on hard times, however, as the writer mentions seeing him at a later date begging with his basket under a bridge in the locality.

The Romanian Word for 'Devil'

Abraham, or 'Bram', Stoker, best remembered as the author of *Dracula*, was born at 15 Marino Crescent, Fairview, in November 1847. The third of seven children, his father was a civil servant at Dublin Castle. As a child, Bram Stoker suffered from ill health; he spent the first eight years of his life in bed, as he was unable to walk or even stand.

One of the earliest influences on Stoker was his mother, Charlotte Thornley, who regaled him with horrific tales of the 1832 cholera epidemic in her native Sligo. One tale that particularly affected the young Stoker was his mother's story of a traveller who was struck down with cholera some distance from the town. The locals, fearing for their own safety, pushed the stranger into a pit with long sticks and buried him alive.

By the time he attended Trinity College in 1864, Stoker had grown out of his childhood illnesses, and he became an athlete of some note. He was also president of the Philosophical Society and Auditor of the Historical Society. On graduation, he entered the civil service but soon found that it was not to his liking. He became interested in the theatre and worked as an unpaid theatre critic for the *Dublin Evening Mail*.

In 1876, when the famous actor Sir Henry Irving played Hamlet in Dublin, Stoker reviewed the play for the newspaper. Irving was impressed, and extended him an invitation to become manager of the Lyceum Theatre in London.

Stoker married his neighbour, the one-time girlfriend of Oscar Wilde, Florence Balcombe, at St Ann's Church in

Dawson Street in 1878. The couple moved to London and Stoker took up Irving's offer. The two became firm friends and Stoker remained at the Lyceum for the next thirty years, managing the day-to-day running of the theatre and acting as Irving's personal secretary.

Stoker's first novel was a little-known work entitled *The Duties of Clerks of Petty Sessions in Ireland*. His most famous book, *Dracula*, published in 1897, was inspired by the classic vampire tale *Carmilla*, written twenty-five years earlier, by another Dubliner, Sheridan Le Fanu. Stoker began research on the Dracula story in 1890. He had originally entitled the book *Count Wampyr* but later changed it to *Dracula*, the Romanian word for 'devil'.

Unfortunately for Stoker, the book was not popular with the British public and it didn't sell many copies. Although it sold well in America, Stoker had neglected to secure the copyright, so he didn't receive a penny for his efforts.

In terms of sales, *Dracula* has made Bram Stoker one of the best-selling authors of all time: *Dracula* lies at Number 2 in the all-time best-sellers list, with the Bible in the Number 1 slot. Over the years, Stoker's book has been the basis for countless films and has spawned a huge industry.

Following the death of his friend Irving in 1906, Stoker published his *Personal Reminiscences of Henry Irving*, and in 1911 his last book, *The Lair of the White Worm*, appeared. He fell into ill health shortly afterwards and died in poverty on 20 April 1912. He was buried at Golders Green cemetery in London.

THE BATTLE OF RATHMINES

The south Dublin suburb of Ranelagh was known in earlier times as Colon or Nova Colonia. The area was one of the royal manors belonging to the archbishop of Dublin and was largely covered by a great forest. The area was accordingly known as Colon's Wood or Cullenswood until the eighteenth century, when it changed to its present name of Ranelagh.

During the early part of the thirteenth century, Dublin was populated by English settlers from Bristol. In 1209 on Easter Monday 500 of the settlers, while engaged in their annual sports day, were massacred by the O'Tooles at Cullenswood. For many years afterwards, the colonists commemorated 'Black Monday' by riding heavily armed, and in great numbers, out to Cullenswood carrying a 'black standard' to 'dare the Irish enemie' to come out and fight them.

During the eighteenth century, the principal residence in Cullenswood was Willbrook House, home of the bishop of Raphoe and Derry. After his death in 1768 the house was sold to a London organ builder who wanted to turn it into a theatre and pleasure garden. He modelled the venture on the famous Ranelagh Gardens in London. Although the enterprise didn't last for too long, it was a popular place of entertainment for Dubliners and the name soon came to be applied to the entire district.

The district of Rathmines was originally known as Meone's Rath after the De Meones family, who came to Ireland in 1279 as part of the entourage of Archbishop John de

Derlington. As the name implies, there was an ancient rath in the area but little is known about its origin. Prior to the arrival of the De Meones family, the lands surrounding this rath were in the possession of Richard de Welton.

The summer of 1649 saw the beginning of the last major battle to take place in Dublin until 1916. The celebrated Battle of Rathmines saw the final defeat of the marquis of Ormonde's Royalist army by the Parliamentarian forces commanded by Colonel Michael Jones, governor of Dublin. The battle began on 1 August when Ormonde sent his men out from his headquarters at Rathmines Castle (near Palmerston Park) to occupy Baggotrath castle at Upper Baggot Street. Jones deployed his own forces to check Ormonde's progress and a full-scale battle quickly ensued. The Royalists were routed and speedily forced out of their stronghold at Rathmines, which was said to be 'well furnished with provisions of victuals, store of wine, silks and velvet, scarlet and other cloth'. In addition, the fleeing Royalists had abandoned 200 oxen and their entire arsenal of weapons and ammunition. Ormonde himself barely managed to evade the clutches of the Parliamentarians by jumping a ditch on his horse.

The lands at Rathgar became the property of a well-known Dublin merchant family, the Cusacks, in 1609, when they bought the castle there for use as a country residence. John Cusack was Lord Mayor of Dublin in 1608 and his son Robert succeeded him in the post. He also served as Sheriff of Dublin during the troubled civil-war years of the mid-seventeenth century. The Cusacks suffered during the rebellion. Royalist soldiers took over their lands, stealing corn and timber and commandeering horses and carts. During the Battle of Rathmines the estate was used as a refuge by the retreating royalist army. After the war, the Cusacks were allowed to keep their estates. By the time of the restoration, however, the family's fortunes had diminished significantly. A 1659 census shows that only the Cusack family, consisting of John and Alice and their two children, along with four servants, remained on the lands. Two of the servants were women and were described as 'a little short wench' and 'a full fat wench.' The only other residents on the estate were described as 'two poor women'.

A Refuge for Unfortunate Females

Arabella Denny, born Arabella Fitzmaurice, second daughter of Thomas, First Earl of Kerry, and Anne Petty in 1707, was the proprietor of the first Magdalen Asylum to be established in Ireland – in 1765 at 8 Lower Leeson Street. The Asylum was established to provide a refuge for 'unfortunate females abandoned by their seducers and rejected by their friends.'

All the inmates of this institution were Protestant women under the age of twenty. The asylum was funded by collections taken at the weekly sermons in the chapel attached to the building. Due to its proximity to the big houses on Stephen's Green, the chapel attracted subscriptions and donations from the wealthiest members of society. Access to the Sunday sermons was by ticket only; the charges were one shilling for the morning service and sixpence for the evening. Tickets were as hard to come by as All-Ireland tickets are today, as the Magdalen chapel attracted to its Sunday services some of the best-known orators of the day. Extraordinary scenes were witnessed on some occasions, with ticket-holders storming the doors of the chapel and jumping over the pews in order to get the best vantage points.

The Magdalen Asylum and chapel were eventually taken over by the Irish Sugar Company. The award-winning eight-storey building now located on the site of the Asylum was erected in 1964.

Arabella Denny spent the latter part of her life at Peafield Cliff in Blackrock, where she is said to have introduced the silkworm to Ireland and set up a silk-weaving business from her home-produced cocoons. Thanks to these efforts, she was elected patron of the Royal Dublin Society's Silk Warehouse in 1765. The following year she was made an honorary member of the society, becoming one of the first women ever to receive this distinction.

Lady Denny had a great fear of being buried alive and left detailed instructions to ensure that this would not happen. In her will, she wrote: 'With regard to my own person, my own desires are very moderate: that I may not be buried until I am certainly dead. I desire that I may be permitted to lie on my bed for at least seventy-two hours or longer.' She directed that after this period – and on confirmation from her doctors that she was definitely dead – her body was to be first encased in a lead coffin and then placed in an oak coffin and taken to her native Kerry for burial.

She died at her home in Blackrock on 18 March 1792 at the age of eighty-five. Her death had been mistakenly announced seven years earlier; this incident probably accounts for her fear of being buried alive. She made provision for a hearse and mourning coach containing two of her servants and two coach drivers to take her remains to her last resting place, in Tralee. She provided the servants and drivers with sufficient expenses for fourteen days, which in those days was considered the norm for a round trip from Dublin to Tralee.

THE ROYAL EXCHANGE

City Hall, which stands at the top of Cork Hill beside Dublin Castle, has served as the meeting place for Dublin Corporation since 1852. The City Hall began life, however, as the Royal Exchange. It was built by the Dublin Guild of Merchants in the 1770s. The merchants petitioned parliament for a plot of land on Cork Hill to build an Exchange in order to enhance the trade and commercial life of the city. Their request was granted and they were given a hundred-square-foot plot of land at the junction of Parliament Street and Dame Street.

Work began on the site in 1768, and the edition of *Faulkner's Journal* for July of that year recorded that workmen commenced the demolition of some old buildings on Cork Hill in order to prepare the ground for the Royal Exchange. One newspaper informed the public that the trustees intended to erect a 'covered building' on the site, as it would be 'most suitable to our climate'! While this work was taking place, a large human skull was unearthed. A tooth extracted from the skull was said at the time to be 'the largest ever seen in this kingdom'.

The site was bought for £13,500 and the building was estimated by John Gilbert to have cost a total of £40,000, which the merchants raised through a series of lotteries. The design and location of the new building raised the hackles of many eighteenth-century Dubliners. One letter-writer to the *Freeman's Journal* complained about the cost of the project at a time when the 'life-blood of the nation is being sucked by a shoal of lazy leeches, that are almost bursting with over-gorged pernicious pensions.' Another writer wanted to know why the Exchange was to be built 'amongst brothels and coal-yards'.

A competition for the design of the Exchange was held, and sixty-one entries were received. The contract was awarded to a then-unknown London-born architect, Thomas Cooley, who died within five years of the completion of the building.

The Royal Exchange eventually opened in 1779 but it was not always used for the purpose for which it had been built. During the 1798 rebellion, the yeomanry used the Exchange as a military HQ and many rebel prisoners were confined and tortured there. One writer made the observation at the time that prisoners would sometimes be sent on their way with a heavy beating, while those less fortunate 'would be ornamented with a pitch-cap, with which he galloped through the silent streets until the flame expired for want of fuel'.

In 1811, a newspaper editor named Watty Cox was placed in the pillory at the Royal Exchange after he had published seditious material in his *Irish Magazine*. It was said that while a crowd of twenty thousand people turned up to view this spectacle, Cox did not receive 'any indignity' from them.

On 24 April 1842, nine people were killed and many more seriously injured when a crowd gathered on a balustrade at the front of the Exchange to witness the pillorying of a local criminal. The balustrade collapsed under the weight of the spectators; those standing directly underneath bore the brunt of the injuries.

In 1851, the Royal Exchange was taken over by Dublin Corporation; from that time on it was known as the City Hall. The Corporation carried out extensive repairs and alterations to the building. One of its first acts was to prevent Jameson Distillers from storing their whiskey in the vaults. The first meeting of Dublin Corporation at the revamped Exchange took place on 30 September 1852.

THE CUSTOMS HOUSE

Dublin's first Customs House – said to have been in use since the mid-thirteenth century – was located at the Crane of Dublin, at the bottom of Winetavern Street. This was the site of the 'Great Explosion' in 1597, in which 126 people were killed and scores wounded when 150 barrels of gunpowder were accidentally ignited.

The Old Customs House, which stood close to what is now Parliament Street, was built in 1620, when James I took a ninety-year lease on a plot of land owned by Jacob Newman. The lease stated that the land was to be used for 'the convenient loading, landing, putting aboard or on shore merchandise as should at any time thereafter be exported or imported.'

In 1707, a new Customs House was erected on the site where the Clarence Hotel now stands. This building, designed by the architect Thomas Burgh, was a three-storey structure made from brick, and its main entrances were in Essex Street and Temple Bar. The new Customs House proved inadequate for the job, however, as the quay in front of it was too small. In fact, it was able to accommodate only four small ships at any given time. Moreover, it was too far away from the mouth of the Liffey, and larger cargoes had to be transferred upriver on flat-bottomed barges or by horse and cart to the building.

As the seventeenth century progressed, it became apparent that the Customs House was an unacceptable landing place for the shipowners: many of them chose to bypass the port altogether by unloading their goods in the shallow waters of Dublin Bay just beyond Ringsend. There was a proposal to build a larger quay at the Customs House in 1753, but by that time moves were already afoot to construct a new building at a more convenient location, closer to the mouth of the river.

The old building was condemned as unsafe in 1773, and the following year the Irish House of Commons decided 'that it will be expedient to build a new Customs House eastward of Batchelor's Lane.'

Initially there was strong opposition to the proposed move from various sections of the Dublin population. Many of the Dublin merchants whose premises were close to the old Customs House felt that the act of moving it to a new location downriver would devalue their properties. People living in the then-posh houses at Gardiner Street and Mountjoy Square were against the new location because they too believed that their properties would be devalued.

In their petition to Parliament, these eighteenth-century NIMBYs voiced their concerns 'that all the hurry, crowd and annoyance which necessarily attend trade will be brought even to the doors of our nobility and gentry, and many of those elegant streets in which they now reside will become the common passages for porters and cars . . . '

All attempts to prevent the move were overcome, however, and the decision to move to the new site was finally made by John Beresford, chief commissioner of the revenue. He laid the foundation stone for the new building in August 1781.

The building of the new Customs House – designed by Gandon – proceeded at a slow pace and was not completed for ten years. During that time, Gandon was forced to contend with strikes, rioting and problems caused by the muddy ground. He was even forced to wear a sword while working because his life had been threatened on several occasions. The Customs House eventually opened for business in 1791 and is now generally regarded as one of the city's finest buildings.

'Saved by the Gallows'

From the sixteenth to the nineteenth centuries, the practice of duelling was very common among the upper classes of European society. Nowhere was it more prevalent than in Dublin. The 'Duel of Honour' was the favoured method among the 'quality' of Dublin for settling disputes, while for others – such as the types that frequented the Hellfire and Abduction clubs – it was just another form of entertainment.

From the early 1700s onward, the flintlock pistol became the favoured weapon of the duellists. Two of the main pistol manufacturers in Dublin at that time were Thomas Fowler of Capel Street and John and William Rigby. Duels were generally fought to local duelling rules. In 1777, however, the Irish 'Code of Duelling' was adopted at Clonmel Assizes as the national standard. The code, also known as 'The Twenty-six Commandments' was drawn up by the duelling fraternity of Galway, Mayo, Sligo, Roscommon and Tipperary. The Phoenix Park was a favoured venue for Dublin duellists, while Clontarf Wood, 'where men of heat go to bleed one another in duels', was a popular spot. The North Bull Strand at Dollymount was also used as a battleground by the 'blazers'.

In 1800 Ballsbridge was the scene of a duel between Henry Grattan and his one-time friend Isaac Corry. Corry had abused Grattan during a debate on the Act of Union and Grattan had retaliated, tearing Corry's reputation to shreds in the process. Corry challenged Grattan to a duel, which took place the following morning. The sheriff attempted to have the duel stopped but he was pushed into a ditch by Corry's second.

At the signal, both men fired and Corry fell down wounded. Grattan was unscathed. He said afterwards that he could have killed Corry but deliberately fired wide.

Daniel O'Connell, 'the Liberator', once took up the duelling pistols to preserve his honour, despite his abhorrence of bloodshed. In 1815, he fought a duel with a member of the Orange-controlled Dublin Corporation named John D'Esterre. O'Connell was forced into the duel after D'Esterre had pursued him around the streets of Dublin with a horsewhip for the best part of a week. A duel was eventually arranged; it took place in front of a large crowd at a spot near Naas on 2 February 1815. D'Esterre fired the first shot and missed. O'Connell then fired, shooting D'Esterre through the bladder. Despite prompt attention from a surgeon, D'Esterre died the following day. O'Connell was afterwards filled with remorse for the killing of D'Esterre. He offered to pay the dead man's widow a pension but she refused to accept it. O'Connell often had to pass the D'Esterre household on Bachelor's Walk on his way from his home to the Four Courts, and he was sometimes seen to stop briefly and raise his hat as he passed the door.

Another famous duel was fought between the informer Leonard McNally and his Harcourt Street neighbour Jonah Barrington. Barrington shot McNally, who fell to the ground and cried out, 'I'm hit!' The doctor in attendance rushed to McNally's aid and quickly discovered that the ball had hit the buckle of his gallows (gallows was a common term at that time for suspenders). The doctor exclaimed, 'By Jaysus, Mac! You are the only rogue I ever knew that was saved by the gallows.'

DUNSINK OBSERVATORY

When Francis Andrews, Provost of Trinity College, died in 1774, he left a legacy of £3,000 for the erection of an astronomical and meteorological observatory at Dunsink. The construction of the observatory began at the end of 1782, and it was open for business three years later. The site at Dunsink was chosen by the first astronomer of the observatory, Henry Usher, for its clear view of the horizon on all sides. It was also selected because it was close enough to the city for the convenience of the students, yet far enough away from the smog produced by the city to benefit from clear skies.

The observatory itself was a two-storey structure with a dome to house the main telescope. There was a house with stables and a garden for the astronomer, and a smaller house for the use of the assistant astronomer. Although a great deal of attention had been paid to the layout of the observatory, the same cannot be said for the water supply. A deep well had been dug, but it was often contaminated by sewage. No action was taken to rectify the problem until an astronomer died from typhoid fever.

Although Ussher had taken great care to build the observatory in a location with an unhindered view of the heavens, there was consternation in 1882 when it was realised that a tree on an adjoining property belonging to a Mr Rathborne would block the viewing of the once-in-a-lifetime spectacle of the planet Venus moving across the sun. The problem was solved when Mr Rathborne had the offending tree cut down.

Dunsink Observatory was for nearly forty years home to the world-famous mathematician William Rowan Hamilton. Hamilton was born at midnight on 3 August 1805 at Number 29 Dominic Street in Dublin. His early schooling was provided by his uncle, a clergyman, at Trim in County Meath. Hamilton was a child prodigy and by the age of four it was said that he would amuse his uncle's dinner guests 'by reading for them equally well whether the book was turned upside down or held in any other fashion.' When he was four and a half, his mother described Hamilton's academic prowess in a letter to her sister. 'His reciting is astonishing and his clear and accurate knowledge of geography is beyond belief,' she wrote. 'He even draws the countries with a pencil on paper, and will cut them out, though not perfectly accurate, yet so well that anybody knowing the countries could not mistake them; but you will think this nothing when I tell you that he reads Latin, Greek and Hebrew.' By the age of twelve, he had a good knowledge of thirteen languages.

It was in the field of mathematics, however, that Hamilton made his mark. In 1827, when he was only twenty-two years old, he was appointed professor of astronomy and superintendent of Dunsink Observatory. He also held the post of Astronomer Royal of Ireland. Hamilton also fancied himself as a poet and entertained many famous poets, including William Wordsworth, Speranza (Oscar Wilde's mother) and Aubrey de Vere, during his forty years at Dunsink. He died at Dunsink on 2 September 1865.

GANGS OF THE LIBERTIES

During the Middles Ages, there were approximately twenty-five areas known as the Liberties or Franchises of Dublin outside the walls of the medieval city of Dublin. All the Liberty areas were outside the control of the Lord Mayor of Dublin and had a certain degree of independence in legal and financial matters.

The main Liberty areas were the Liberty of St Sepulchre, which was under the control of the Archbishop of Dublin, the Liberty of St Patrick, and the Liberties of Thomas Court and Donore, which belonged to the Abbey of St Thomas. The other Liberty areas of Dublin were located at Ballybough, Clonskeagh, Clontarf, Dolphin's Barn, Donnybrook, Drumcondra, Finglas, Grangegorman, Milltown, Stoneybatter, Raheny and Ringsend.

Today, however, the name applies only to the inner-city area to the south and west of the walls of the old city. This area was at one time the most important part of the city for the manufacturing industry. In particular, the Liberties were traditionally associated with the textile and silk industries that flourished there until the end of the seventeenth century.

For most of the eighteenth century, rioting was a common occurrence on the streets of Dublin; one of the most formidable street gangs was that of the 'Liberty Boys'. It was a Protestant gang, and its members were mainly weavers from the Coombe. Their main rivals were the Catholic 'Ormond Boys', who were butchers from the Ormond Market. The weavers and butchers fought each

111

other regularly at weekends throughout the century, but in 1748 the rioting reached new levels of intensity. The summer months of that year saw some of the heaviest fighting, with the two gangs clashing nearly every night in the area around Camden Street and Aungier Street. In August, the *Dublin Courant* newspaper reported on a riot in the Phoenix Park between the two factions. The report recounts the capture of one of the butchers by the Liberty Boys. They tied a rope around his neck, with the intention of hanging him from a tree, but were prevented from doing so by their own leader. The report does not make clear whether the man was killed in the incident, but it does state that he was 'hacked in so terrible a manner that he is past giving any further disturbance to the public'. The Ormond Boys retaliated soon afterwards when they hung one of the weavers from St Audeon's Gate from meat hooks.

The butchers' violent activities often took them beyond the confines of the city. On St Stephen's Day in 1787, a large group travelled out to Finglas, to go bull-baiting with their dogs. Unable to find a bull, the butchers spent the day drinking instead. On returning to the city later in the day, they became violent and attacked some local people at Finglas Bridge. During the riot that followed, two people were killed and many others badly injured. The butchers attacked the home of James McClean, and during the ensuing struggle McClean was stabbed with a bayonet by a butcher named David Bobbit. Bobbit himself was killed by a Finglas man wielding a slash hook. The butchers were chased out of the house and a violent mêlée broke out on the bridge; a man by the name of Tom Legget was hacked to death with a sword.

The St Stephen's Day bull-baiting contest was an annual event in those times and it was invariably followed by violence. In 1789, the city sheriff, backed up by a heavy military force, attempted to break up a bullfight in a field near the Customs House at the bottom of Abbey Street. They marched into the middle of the arena, ordered the onlookers to disperse and arrested eight of their number. The arrests inflamed the crowd and they quickly surrounded the soldiers, hurling stones and oyster shells at them. The sheriff ordered his men to fire on the unarmed rioters and four of them were shot dead. One at the Customs House was unnamed, while three men – Patrick Keegan, James Mahassey and Farrell Reddy – were killed in Abbey Street.

Despite their intense rivalry, the gangs collaborated in one of the most gruesome incidents of that period. They joined forces to deal with a notorious Dublin criminal named Paul 'Gallows' Farrell, who had upset both gangs. Farrell was kidnapped by the Ormond Boys, who carried him up to the Liberties, where they joined forces with their deadly enemies. The *Dublin Evening Post* of 24 August 1734 reported that the mob 'began to lay violent hands on him . . . they cut him in several parts of the head and body and deprived him of one of his testicles.' The unfortunate Farrell was then dragged through the streets to Chamber Street (near Ardee Street), where he was hanged from a tree.

During the latter years of the eighteenth century, when industrial violence was rife in the city, a group known as the Liberty Light Horsemen gained control of the Dublin journeymen tailor's council. This group first came to the attention of the public in 1789 when it organised a riot involving over a hundred tailors that resulted in the deaths of a policeman and a tailor. Two members of the Liberty Light Horsemen named Thomas McDermott and John Read were hanged in front of Newgate Prison in 1790 for an attack on a timber yard in Spitalfields. Two years later, several members of the Horsemen, including their leader, Charles

Wall, were arrested during an assault on a master clothier at his home in Weaver's Square. Wall was sentenced to transportation, while the rest of the gang was sentenced to six months in jail and a whipping from Cork Street to Weaver's Square and back.

ELEPHANT LANE

Luke Gardiner, the wealthy banker and Dublin MP, was responsible for the development of large chunks of the north side of Dublin city in the eighteenth century. Gardiner bought lands at Mary's Abbey, Moore Street, Henry Street, Earl Street and Drogheda Street, which was later renamed Sackville Street and subsequently became O'Connell Street.

Gardiner first developed Henrietta Street, which at one time contained some of the finest houses on the north side of the city. During the late 1740s, he turned his attention to Drogheda Street, which was then a narrow thoroughfare running from Parnell Street to Abbey Street on what is now the eastern side of O'Connell Street. He demolished all the original buildings on the street and replaced them with imposing town houses. He doubled the width of the street to 150 feet and erected a tree-lined mall in the centre. The mall was fifty feet wide and 700 feet long and was enclosed by a small wall. Inside the wall there was a pathway lined with elm trees. The mall itself was called Gardiner's Mall and the rest of the street was renamed Sackville Street, after Lionel Caulfield Sackville, First Duke of Dorset and Lord Lieutenant of Ireland from 1731 to 1737 and from 1751 to 1755.

At that time Sackville Street was the premier thoroughfare in Ireland and was described in some quarters as the finest street in the world. It was improved further in 1772 by the Wide Street Commissioners, who made grants available for development of the ground between Upper Sackville Street and the River Liffey. The work at Lower Sackville Street was nearly complete by 1789 and in 1792 the street was connected to the burgeoning south side of the city with the addition of Carlisle Bridge. The bridge was not a success, however, and by 1824 it was in need of major refurbishment. By 1852 it was in a very dangerous state and the Earl of Charlemont described it as 'the most dangerous in the Empire'.

Carlisle Bridge was replaced in 1880 by the present O'Connell Bridge. The new bridge caused some controversy as the Dublin Port and Docks Board wanted to retain the old name, while Dublin Corporation insisted that it be named after 'the Liberator', Daniel O'Connell. The Corporation won the day, and five years later they passed a resolution renaming Sackville Street as O'Connell Street.

Cathedral Street, leading from O'Connell Street to Marlborough Street, was once colourfully known as Elephant Lane. The origin of the name is unclear but it is possible that there was a menagerie close to the lane in the eighteenth century. One writer says that the name came about because a large elephant was burned to death there in 1681, but this incident actually occurred in Essex Street. The elephant was taken to Dublin for an exhibition, and on the night of 17 June 1681 the stable where he was being kept caught fire and the elephant died. Large crowds gathered at the scene, and when the fire was extinguished they proceeded to take parts of the elephant away as souvenirs. The remains of the elephant were dissected by a Doctor Mullen, who preserved the skeleton and sent it to London. Mullen complained afterwards about the Dublin butchers who had assisted him in his task, saying that they were too quick to 'cut and slash what came first in their way, and their unruliness did hinder me from making several remarks which otherwise I would have made.' The events of that night were commemorated in the name of the popular 'Elephant Tavern', which traded in Essex Street for many years afterwards.

THE GLASS BOTTLE PLANT

The closure of the former Irish Glass Bottle Plant at Ringsend in 2002, with the loss of nearly four hundred jobs, was a serious blow to an industry that has survived at Ringsend for over two hundred years.

In 1787, the first glass plant was established at Charlotte Quay in Ringsend. The *Dublin Chronicle* newspaper of 22 September 1787 carried an article announcing the establishment of the new glass factory: 'The demand for glass for the French market has encouraged a wealthy company from England to build a glass-house in the neighbourhood of this city. The situation they have chosen is at the foot of Ringsend Bridge.' Most of their wares were indeed manufactured for the French market. They did not supply this market for very long, however, as the trade was adversely affected by the French Revolution and the Napoleonic Wars.

The village (as it was then) continued to be attractive to glass manufacturers, however. Firstly, there was no export duty on Irish glass. The tax on English glass manufacturers had doubled in 1777 and four years later it had increased even further. Secondly, glass-making was a major coal-consuming industry and tax was not levied on the importation of coal when it was used in the manufacture of glass. As they were heavily coal-reliant, the glass factories were a major source of pollution and smog in the area, which led one writer to describe Ringsend as 'an unchangeably wretched village', while another was moved to call the village 'a sink of filth'.

Ringsend also had a natural advantage because of its

coastal location. Nearby there was an abundance of sand, which constituted 80 per cent of the material needed to make bottles. Another major advantage was its proximity to the port of Dublin.

Glass workers came from far and wide to work in Ringsend; they included a large Scottish contingent. In time, they too, like the Torbay fishermen before them, became an important part of life in Ringsend. The glass-workers usually worked twelve-hour shifts, from 6 AM to 6 PM. At 4.30 every morning, a man employed by the glass factories would go around the homes of the workers and tap on their bedroom windows with a twenty-foot pole to wake them up!

A bottle-making crew consisted of five men sitting in a circle around a conical-shaped funnel called a 'flasher'. The bottle-maker himself was the head man of the crew, the gatherer took the glass from the tank, the servitor blew the bottle, the wetter-off removed the bottle from its mould, and the boy was responsible for the stacking of the bottles in a bottle arch. The glass-workers kept themselves to themselves. As the men were cooped up for long hours in the stifling atmosphere of the glass factories, they were instantly recognisable around Ringsend by their pale complexions. The factories were generally 'closed shops' and usually only bottle-makers' sons were admitted as apprentices.

According to *Alexander Thom's Directory* for 1852, the glass factories operating in Ringsend during the middle of the nineteenth century included Martin Crean's of Fitzwilliam Quay and a plant owned by the Reverend John Prior. Elija Pring opened a factory towards the end of the nineteenth century; this afterwards became known as the Ringsend Bottle Company. Others were the Hibernian Bottle Company, King Brothers Bottleworks and the Crib.

KILL OR CURE

The lands at Harold's Cross once belonged to the powerful Anglo-Norman Harold family, whose main stronghold was at Harold's Grange in Rathfarnham. Harold's Cross at that time bordered the Archbishop of Dublin's manor of St Sepulchre. From early times, the archbishop maintained a gallows on the green, where the park is now located; the boundary between the two areas was marked with a cross.

As it was on the main route from the city to the mountains above Rathfarnham, Harold's Cross was known during the fourteenth century as 'the Pass'. Ball gives alternative names for the area, such as Campus Sancti Patricii and Russel Rath. The former name might have some merit, as there was a legend associating St Patrick with the area. There was another tale in circulation in ancient times claiming that the stones used in the construction of St Patrick's Cathedral came from a quarry at Harold's Cross.

The village green was the focal point of Harold's Cross until the late nineteenth century. The first inhabitants of the green were described as squatters; they built mud cabins there and raised pigs, chickens and goats. There was also a maypole on the green and the maidens of the village danced around it in summertime. In 1836, the tavern owners of Harold's Cross, in an attempt to revive the old custom of holding May sports on the green, donated a new maypole to the village. Despite their efforts, the new sports never really caught on, and they were abandoned a few years later.

During the eighteenth and nineteenth centuries, Harold's Cross was a popular resort for recovering invalids. The area was also referred to as 'Kill-or-cure' by the citizens, because large numbers of patients in the last stages of illness attended the hospital there, where they would either die or be cured. Harold's Cross had also gained a reputation as a sanatorium for sick children, as many Dubliners sent their ailing children there to be nursed in a pollution-free environment. The parents usually spent Sundays with their children, where 'they were wont to repair hither to spend the day, and dine in rustic fashion on bacon and chickens.' Over a period of time, some of the parents bought run-down cabins in Harold's Cross and built new houses on the sites. In time, this led to the area becoming a suburb of the city. Burton described Harold's Cross at that time as a 'community of reflecting, sober families. Independents of Cromwell's school, and many of the respectable members of the Society of Friends, made this their peaceful abode.'

Following Robert Emmet's ill-fated rebellion of 1803, Dublin was inundated with corps of yeomen, and the area of Harold's Cross was no exception. The official name of the local militia was the Upper Cross Fusiliers. This corps was taken from the ranks of the working class; they were given the derisory name 'the Upper Crust Fusiliers' by their better-off contemporaries.

Two Harold's Cross sisters known as the Kinnegad Slashers were familiar faces on the streets of Dublin during the 1820s and 1830s. The sisters were described as dressing in flaming crimson and stepping out 'like two grenadiers'. Another resident of Harold's Cross, Nathaniel Burton, defended their character in a letter, saying that, contrary to popular opinion, the women were of good character and were 'very well conducted'. When one of the sisters died, Burton, rather strangely, supposed that she had expired from 'the extreme lightness of her dress, and tightening her stays too much, to form a slender waist'!

Another well-known figure in Harold's Cross at that time was the dairymaid who was given the name Peggy-the-Man because she wore a man's hat and overcoat. Peggy was often seen carrying milk pails around the village or on her knees praying in a secluded spot.

KING OF THE DUBLIN BEGGARS

On 8 November 1773, the House of Industry in North Brunswick Street threw open its doors to the poor of Dublin for the first time. Four months earlier, the *Hibernian Journal* announced that 'two large and commodious houses' on eleven acres of ground had been purchased by Dublin Corporation in Channel Row (North Brunswick Street) to house 'the badged as well as other strolling beggars, whereby the citizens will be effectually relieved from a nuisance and disgrace that has long attended this metropolis.' In 1772, the problem of begging was so acute in Dublin that under an Act of Parliament it was decided to issue metal badges to beggars in an effort to regulate their numbers. Only the holders of these badges were allowed to solicit for alms in the city streets.

The House of Industry, which effectively became a poorhouse, consisted of the Richmond, Hardwicke and Whitworth Hospitals. It also contained an asylum for the aged and infirm poor, an asylum for incurable lunatics and the Bedford Asylum for the reception of children. It was run by a board of governors and was mainly supported by charitable bodies, through government aid and by subscription from the city's merchant and professional classes.

The day-to-day running of the house was carried out by a group that included surgeons, superintendents, nurses and housekeepers. At the bottom of the scale were the beadles, whose task it was to 'preserve order and regularity in the halls at the hours of breakfast, dinner &c.'

Another of the beadles' tasks was to travel the city in the

'black cart' to take in by force beggars who were reluctant to enter the house under their own steam. These expeditions usually met with violent resistance from the beggars, and beadles were often badly injured in such incidents. After the killing of a head beadle during a riot in the late 1780s, the board of governors decided to arm the beadles with pistols and bayonets. Twenty years later, they were equipped with carbines and swords.

One of the best-known Dublin beggars to end up in the House of Industry was Patrick Corrigan, described as the 'King of the Dublin Beggars' or, to give him his correct title, 'His Lowness, Prince Hackball'. Corrigan was often to be seen travelling through the city on his little cart, drawn by two dogs, to his usual begging spot on the Old Bridge at Church Street. Many attempts were made over the years to incarcerate Corrigan in the House of Industry. He was in fact captured in 1744 by the parish beadle of St Werburgh's Church but was rescued by his friends. He was eventually caught in Parkgate Street by a silk weaver, who carried him single-handedly all the way to Channel Row.

Another Dublin beggar, the infamous Billy-in-the-Bowl from Stoneybatter, was an early resident of the House of Industry. In 1774, the board of governors decided that 'the man in the bowl dish is not a proper person to be discharged from the House of Industry.' Billy must have managed to get out somehow because he was sentenced to life imprisonment for murder twelve years later.

The central part of the House of Industry was taken over in 1838 by the Poor Law commissioners, and it was known thereafter as the North Dublin Union Workhouse.

DUNSOGHLY CASTLE

The building used as Edinburgh Castle in the film epic *Braveheart*, starring Mel Gibson, is actually the fifteenth-century Dunsoghly Castle, which stands about three miles north-west of Finglas, just off the road to Slane. The castle, described as 'one of the finest tower houses in the country', with its four corner turrets, is unique in Ireland for the survival of its trussed-oak roof. The castle was transformed for the *Braveheart* scenes by the addition of battlements, a drawbridge and a great hall.

Dunsoghly Castle was built by the Plunkett family during the mid-fifteenth century and is believed to stand on the site of the original *dún* (fort) which gives the area its name. There was a small chapel adjoining the castle; Joyce, in his *Neighbourhood of Dublin*, mentions the remains of a small brewery there in 1912.

The building of Dunsoghly Castle is attributed to Sir Rowland Plunkett, who was mentioned in connection with the building in 1446. One hundred years later, while John Plunkett was in residence at the castle, it was one of his duties to provide food and lodgings for the Lord Deputy, Sir Edward Bellingham. In a letter to Plunkett, Bellingham chastised him for the poor quality of beer he served and also ordered him to procure new beds for him and his retainers in time for their next visit. The same John Plunkett was responsible for the building of the little chapel adjoining the castle. There is an unusual stone plaque fixed into the wall over the door of the chapel that bears John Plunkett's initials;

the date on the plaque is 1573. The plaque represents the Crucifixion of Christ and features a whip, a spear, a hammer, nails and a ladder while the central part of the plaque depicts the heart, hands and feet of Christ mounted on a crucifix.

Following John Plunkett's death, Dunsoghly passed into the hands of his grandson Sir Christopher Plunkett, who was described as being a 'gracious and eminent lawyer'. Christopher was an advocate for the rights of Catholics; he got into trouble with the English government in 1609 when he sent one of his sons to the Continent to be educated for the priesthood. Someone had falsely claimed that his son had tried to smuggle into Ireland 'a girdle' containing 'popish books and relics'. The allegations did not do Christopher any harm, however, as he was elected a member of parliament four years later. He was summoned to appear in the Star Chamber during that year, after he had spoken out against the oppressive activities of the English military within the Pale.

At the time of the 1641 Rising, Sir Henry Tichbourne was in residency at Dunsoghly. Tichbourne, who had acted as ward to two of the Plunketts, left in 1666, after receiving compensation of £2,000 from the government for losses sustained during the rebellion.

Henry Plunkett, a devout Catholic, and the last of the male line of the Plunketts, died in 1760. In his will he left instructions that six priests and 'almswomen' attend his funeral. Just before his death, Henry's younger brother Nicholas also died; Dunsoghly then passed to Nicholas's three daughters, Mary, Catherine and Margaret.

John Dalton, in his *History of the County of Dublin*, says that during the 1830s the castle was in the possession of a Mrs Kavanagh, 'one of the descendants and co-heiresses of Sir John Plunkett'.

The Kingdom of Mud Island

'King of Mud Island' was the dubious title bestowed on the leader of a seventeenth-century band of highwaymen, smugglers, thieves and outlaws of every kind. This motley crew inhabited an area called Mud Island, close to where the Luke Kelly Bridge now crosses the Tolka river at Ballybough. This colony is believed to have been founded by three brothers named McDonnell who had lost their lands during the Ulster plantations.

There has been a bridge crossing the Tolka at Ballybough for the past seven hundred years. In 1311, a former Lord Mayor of Dublin, John le Decer, built a bridge there to connect the city with Clontarf but it was swept away by floods shortly afterwards. Another bridge was built to replace it and this structure is mentioned in a description of the 'riding of the city franchises' in 1488. The riders, the record tells us, rode 'by the gate of Ballybough to the water of Tolka by the bridge of Ballybough before riding to the sea at Clontarf.'

Seventeenth-century Ballybough was a very different place from the bustling, built-up area that it is today. Back then, it was separated from the city by a large area of open country; it was largely surrounded by water and was accessible by foot only at low tide. Because of its isolation and distance from the long arm of the law, Mud Island soon began to thrive as a smugglers' haven and a refuge for all types of outlaw. The inhabitants of the district even elected their own 'king'. One of these kings, Art Grainger, was killed during a gun battle with customs officers in 1759, while another, 'Grid Iron

McDonnell', once managed to evade the clutches of the sheriff of Dublin by dressing as a woman.

Mud Island was also renowned for its bare-knuckle boxers. The most famous of these was Jack Langan, who featured in many epic brawls on the island.

The island was then, and remained until the 1850s, a place where no law- or excise-man would venture unless accompanied by a substantial back-up force. During that period it was common to find the bodies of revenue officials and excisemen lying in the streets of Mud Island. So common was this occurrence, in fact, that it gave rise to the saying: 'Tis a wise man that never saw a dead one.'

Ballybough, or *Baile Bocht,* 'the town of the poor', was once the location of two unusual burial grounds. The junction where the Clonliffe House pub now stands was a place of burial for suicides two hundred years ago. In those days it was the practice to drive stakes through the bodies of these unfortunate people to prevent their souls from 'wandering abroad at unseemly hours and alarming the public'.

In 1717, the small community of Jews living in Ballybough rented a plot for use as a graveyard. Thirty years later they bought the land outright. They obtained a thousand-year leasehold for the unusual rent of one peppercorn per year. John D'Alton in his *History of County Dublin* gives us an interesting description of the burial rituals in the cemetery: 'Under the head of each corpse is placed a bag of earth, the face is studiously turned towards the east, and the mourners, returning from the grave, pluck the grass and strew it behind them.' This was the only Jewish graveyard in Dublin until 1900; the last burial there was in 1958.

The Carrickmines Massacre

Until significant archaeological discoveries at the medieval Carrickmines Castle were made public, its history was for the most part ignored. The surrounding area has also proved to be of archeological interest. In 1998, during excavations linked to the construction of a Bord Gáis pipeline, a *fulacht fia*, or prehistoric cooking site, was uncovered at Carrickmines Great. The *fulacht fia* comprised two small cooking pits, one of which contained burnt bone. Timber taken from a similar pit in the neighbouring townland of Jamestown has been dated to around 3000 BC.

Carrickmines Castle was built by the Walsh family in the thirteenth century, during the early years of the Anglo-Norman occupation of Ireland. It was one of a series of castles constructed in south Dublin after the conquest to protect the borders of the Pale from the natives who then inhabited the Dublin and Wicklow Mountains. There were other castles close by at Murphystown and Kilgobbin. Carrickmines, however, was the most formidable stronghold in the area, and throughout the fourteenth century there was a substantial garrison stationed there. In 1360, the records show that there was a troop of horsemen operating out of the castle, and in 1375 a large force of men under the command of John Colton, dean of St Patrick's Cathedral, was based there. In 1388, 'forty mounted archers' were billeted at Carrickmines.

Over the course of the centuries, the Walshes had built

up a formidable reputation as fighting men, and they played a vital role in the protection of the Crown's lands within the confines of the Pale. By the end of the sixteenth century, their influence in the area had diminished considerably, and it was recorded that, despite the presence of a large troop of horsemen at Carrickmines, the Wicklow men swept down from the mountains and devastated the surrounding area. The seventeenth century signalled the end of Walsh dominance in the area, and by the time of the 1641 Rebellion the family had switched sides and joined their Irish neighbours in the revolt against the Crown.

During the rebellion of 1641, Carrickmines Castle was taken over by a large party of insurgents and Sir Simon Harcourt was dispatched from Dublin to retake it. This proved easier said than done, and Harcourt was forced to postpone his attack on the castle until reinforcements arrived from the city.

The next day Harcourt fell victim to an Irish sniper within the castle who had already caused great havoc with what was described as 'a long piece that had already done great execution'. Harcourt was shot in the neck and chest and died soon afterwards at Lord Fitzwilliam's castle at Merrion.

Carrickmines was eventually retaken, but not without great loss of life. Harcourt's forces lost about forty men, while the entire complement of rebels within the castle, believed to number about three hundred, and including women and children, was slaughtered. The castle itself was levelled on that occasion.

In the light of the discovery of the remains of several women's bodies at the site, it is very interesting to note a paragraph that originally appeared in Clarendon's *History of the Rebellion and Civil Wars in Ireland*:

After quarter given by Lieutenant-Colonel Gibson to those of the Castle, they were all put to the sword, being about three hundred and fifty, most of them women and children, and Colonel Washington endeavouring to save a pretty child of seven years of age, carried him under his cloak, but the child against his will was killed in his arms, which was a principal motive of him quitting that service.

THE LONG HOLE

Just outside the harbour at Howth in County Dublin lies the small rocky island known as Ireland's Eye. Until the early Christian period, the island was called 'Inish Ereann', or 'Erin's Island'. In the late sixth century, the island came to be known as 'Inish Mac Nessan', after Nessan's three sons established a church there in honour of Saint Maodhóg of Ferns. It was at Nessan's church that the famous *Garland of Howth* was crafted. This beautifully illuminated copy of the Four Gospels was produced by monks on the island some time around the tenth century. It is now preserved in Trinity College.

In September 1852, Ireland's Eye provided the location for a controversial nineteenth-century murder case. Dublin artist William Bourke Kirwan and his wife Maria had spent the summer months of that year in lodgings at Howth. Over the course of the summer, the couple made several trips out to Ireland's Eye, where William spent his time drawing and painting, while Maria, a keen swimmer, whiled away the hours reading and swimming.

The Kirwans were due to return to their city home in Merrion Street on 7 September, and the day before, they decided to take one last boat trip out to Ireland's Eye. The couple arranged with local boatmen Michael and Patrick Nangle to be picked up at 8 PM for the short return journey to Howth. When the Nangles arrived on the island, they were met by William Kirwan, who was alone on the shore.

Kirwan told the men that he hadn't seen Maria since 6

PM, and they set off in different directions to search for her. An hour later, Patrick Nangle discovered her dead body lying in a shallow pool at a place known as the Long Hole. When the body was brought back to Howth, Kirwan insisted that the corpse be washed and laid out, even before it had been examined by the police doctor. The following morning, the coroner made arrangements for a medical examination of the body and a verdict of accidental drowning was established.

Five days later, Maria was buried at Glasnevin Cemetery. Almost immediately afterwards, rumours began to circulate about Kirwan's private life. The police became suspicious of him after it emerged that he had been living a double life. It was established that he had been involved in a secret relationship with a Sandymount woman, Teresa Kenny, by whom he had seven children.

Soon afterwards, seven witnesses came forward claiming to have heard screams coming from Ireland's Eye on the night of the incident. Although there was no hard evidence to link William Kirwan with his wife's death, he was arrested and charged with her murder. The case against Kirwan was based entirely on circumstantial evidence, but he was convicted after a dubious intervention by the trial judge, Mr Justice Crampton. The trial lasted for only two days; at 8 PM on 9 December the jury returned to the court after deliberating for less than an hour and told the judge that they would be unable to agree a verdict that night. Crampton informed them that they would be locked up in the jury room all night without food. This threat seemed to concentrate their minds and they returned with a guilty verdict at 11 PM.

Kirwan was sentenced to death but this was later commuted to life imprisonment on appeal. He served a total of twenty-six years in jail, eight of them in Bermuda and the remainder on Spike Island. He was released on compassionate grounds in 1879, on condition that he leave Ireland forever. He was taken under escort to Cobh (then Queenstown), where he was placed on board a ship bound for America. He was never heard from again.

The Irish Crown Jewels

Frank Shackleton, brother of the polar explorer Ernest, was a prime suspect in one of the great Irish mysteries of the twentieth century. Only days before the arrival of King Edward and Queen Alexandra for a state visit to Ireland in 1907, it was discovered that the Irish crown jewels had vanished without trace from a safe in Dublin Castle.

The Irish crown jewels were officially known as 'the Insignia of the Most Illustrious Order of St Patrick'. The Order had been founded in 1783 by King George III and was the Irish equivalent of the Scottish Order of the Thistle and the English Order of the Garter. The jewels themselves were made in 1830 by the London firm of Rundell and Bridge for ceremonial use by the Lord Lieutenant of Ireland or visiting monarchs. The main pieces in the collection were an eight-pointed star and a badge; these were made from Brazilian rubies, diamonds and emeralds On the star was a Latin inscription that can be translated as: 'Who can separate us?' At the time of their disappearance, the jewels were worth an estimated £40,000. At today's prices, they would be worth well in excess of ¤1 million.

Before 1905, the jewels had been kept in a bank vault; they were taken to the castle only when they were required for ceremonial occasions. In 1905, however, it was decided that the jewels should be placed inside a steel safe in a strongroom at the Office of Arms in the Castle. When the safe arrived at the Castle, it was found to be too big to fit through the doorway and it was placed in the ground-floor library of the Bedford Tower instead.

On 3 July 1907, the office cleaner, Mary Farrell, found the door to the library unlocked and reported the matter to William Stivey, an assistant to Sir Arthur Vicars, Ulster King of Arms. Stivey told Vicars about the problem but Vicars took no action. Three days later, the cleaner found the door open again, this time with the key in the lock. Stivey informed Vicars about the occurrence but again no action was taken. Later that afternoon, while Stivey was returning a gold collar to the safe, he found that it was unlocked. He immediately informed Vicars, who opened the safe – to find that the jewels had disappeared.

Suspicion immediately fell on the head of Frank Shackleton, who was a good friend of Vicars. Shackleton lived at Vicars's house in Clonskeagh Road, and it would have been easy for him to copy the safe key. Just two days before the robbery, he had been heard to remark that he wouldn't be surprised if the jewels were stolen one day. Shackleton was later exonerated by an enquiry into the theft but he was subsequently convicted on a charge of embezzling a widow's life savings. Vicars himself was forced to resign and he retired to Kilmorna House in County Kerry. His house was later burnt down and he was shot dead by the IRA in 1921.

The jewels were never seen again. Rumours persist as to their whereabouts, however. For example, in 1976 there was an intriguing reference to the case when a government file from 1926 came to light. The file refers to William T. Cosgrave, then president of the Irish Free State, who understood that the 'castle jewels are for sale and that they could be got for £2,000 or £3,000.' Other rumours suggested that the jewels were hidden at Three Rock in the Dublin Mountains or in the ruins of Vicars's house in Kerry.

Hoggen Green

During medieval times, the College Green area of Dublin was known variously as Hoggen Green, Hogges Green, Hog's Green and Hogan's Green. Most historical sources agree that the name derives from the convent of St Mary Del Hogges but opinion is divided as to the origins of the 'Hogges' part of the name. It has been suggested that the name means 'St Mary of the Virgins' but Haliday's more convincing explanation in his *Scandinavian Kingdom of Dublin* says it comes from the Viking word 'Hoge' or 'Hoga', meaning mound or burial ground. Over the years, a number of Viking burial mounds have been discovered in this area.

Whatever the origin of the name, the convent itself was built in the mid-twelfth century by Dermot McMurrough, King of Leinster, close to where Trinity College is now situated. Over time, the open ground beside the convent came to be known as Hoggen Green, and for many years it was used as a place for grazing animals, as a recreation ground and as a place of execution.

One of the earliest recorded executions to have taken place on the Green was that of 'Black' Adam O'Toole, who was publicly burned there in the fourteenth century for heresy and for his declaration that the Holy Scriptures were in fact fairy tales.

Also found on the Green at that time was the 'Hoggen Butts', where Dubliners went to practise their archery skills. A form of nine-pin bowling was also played there. The archery butts were mentioned in an act of Parliament in 1465 that decreed that every town under English control in Ireland was to provide 'one pair of butts for shooting within the town or near it, and every man of the same town between the ages of sixteen and sixty shall muster at said butts and shoot up and down three times every feast day.' There had obviously been problems with people stealing clay from the butts. A law passed by the Corporation in 1469 stated: 'No manner of man take no clay from Hogges butts upon pain of twenty shillings as oft as they may be found so doing.'

Hoggen Green was evidently used over a long period of time as a dump for human and animal waste. A city ordinance of 1468 refers to the dumping of dung in 'the holl beyan the Hogges butt', while a similar order one hundred years later commands that 'all dung that shall be carried to the said Hoggen Green shall be placed in the great hole by All Hallows'. This hole was later the site of Trinity College. The Green area later became known as 'Hogg and Butts' and later again as 'Hogan's Green'; the name 'College Green' began to be used during the early nineteenth century.

Close by Hoggen Green was Hog Hill, which is now Andrews Street. During his early days as a lawyer, John Philpott Curran resided at Hog Hill for a time; he claimed that he was so poor while he was living there that 'my wife and children were the chief furniture of my apartments'. He also said at the time that his rent had the same chance of being paid as the national debt! Another Hog Hill resident of renown was the lame cobbler John Travere, who was renowned for his savage wit and sarcasm. Travere regularly drew large crowds to his shoe stand on Hog Hill, where he regaled them with his tales.

MURDER AT LA MANCHA

In April 1926, a large mansion at Malahide was the scene of a horrific multiple murder. The house, known as La Mancha, was located on thirty acres of land on the Malahide Road. Four members of the McDonnell family, originally from Ballygar, County Galway, and two of their servants were poisoned with arsenic and bludgeoned to death. The house was then set on fire. The dead were named as single siblings Annie (58), Joseph (56), Peter (53) and Alice McDonnell (46). The other two deceased were servants Mary McGowan and James Clarke.

The McDonnell home, which was situated opposite the northern end of the grounds of Malahide Castle, was up for sale when it was burned. The McDonnells had bought it six years previously when they retired from their grocery, drapery and general store in Ballygar. Friends said they intended to move nearer Dublin city.

On the morning of 31 March 1926 a fire was discovered in the house by the family's gardener, Henry McCabe. Before the fire brigade got there, one body had been dragged out of the building. Soon afterwards four other bodies were discovered inside. The bodies of Joseph, his sisters Annie and Alice, and Mary McGowan were burnt almost beyond recognition. The body of James Clarke was discovered in the basement; he had been beaten around the head with a blunt instrument. The remains of Peter McDonnell, loosely covered by items of clothing, were found in the dining room.

Initially, the finger of suspicion was pointed at Peter McDonnell. The theory was that he had lost his reason during the night, murdered the entire household and then set fire to the house, killing himself in the process. But this theory was discounted when it was discovered that the clothes had been placed on Peter McDonnell's body after he died. His head bore a number of bruises and a poker was found in the dining room close to his body.

A week after the tragedy the gardaí still had more questions than answers but one man – Henry McCabe – increasingly came under suspicion. In a statement he told the gardaí that family members had been acting strangely with one another and he also claimed that Peter McDonnell seemed 'very abnormal' and used to throw himself on the ground laughing. But he gave the game away when he showed the gardaí some keys he claimed he had found in a pair of Peter's trousers while searching for survivors in the house. One of the keys fitted a safe in the basement, which was found to be empty. There was now a motive for the murder – robbery.

Two weeks later Henry McCabe was formally charged with murder and in November 1926 he went on trial at the Dublin Central Criminal Court. When he failed in his attempt to blame the murders on Peter McDonnell, he tried to cast suspicion on the servant James Clarke. But the prosecution made clear to the jury that everything of any value had been pilfered from La Mancha before it was set on fire.

When convicted of the crime, McCabe whispered, 'I can only say, God forgive you and the people who swore falsely against me. I have been the victim of bribery and perjury.' After he was sentenced to death, a petition for clemency was signed by more than 2,000 people and presented to the Minister for Justice. The effort was in vain. Henry McCabe was hanged at Mountjoy Jail on 9 December 1926.

The Fighting Doctor

Kathleen Florence Lynn, doctor and revolutionary, was born near Cong in County Mayo in 1875. She was the daughter of the Reverend Robert Young Lynn, a Church of Ireland rector. In 1899, she became one of the first women to graduate in medicine from the Royal University of Ireland. She was also the first woman to be elected house surgeon at the Adelaide Hospital in Dublin. Because of her gender, she was discriminated against by the predominantly male medical staff at the hospital. They opposed her appointment and it was never ratified. However, she became a Fellow of the Royal College of Surgeons in 1909 and practised at the Rotunda and Sir Patrick Dun's Hospitals before starting her own private practice at Belgrave Road, Rathmines, in Dublin.

Dr Lynn was a member of the Women's Suffrage Movement and it was through her involvement with this organisation that she became interested in republican politics. She joined the Irish Citizen Army during the 1913 Lockout as a first-aid instructor. After the strike, she became chief medical officer of the Irish Citizen Army and was involved in the preparations for the 1916 Rising. On the weekend of the Rising, she was promoted to the rank of captain by James Connolly.

Lynn was arrested on Easter Monday at City Hall in Dublin after the British found an automatic pistol and fifty rounds of ammunition in her medical bag. She spent brief periods in Kilmainham and Mountjoy Jail. Her friend Countess Markievicz recalled many years later that Dr Lynn had looked after her for a time after her release from jail. She took the countess to her home at 9 Belgrave Road in Rathmines, where, in the countess's own words, 'she welcomed me to her house, where she cared for me and fed me up and looked after me till I had recovered from the evil effects of the English prison system'.

Although Dr Lynn was well ahead of her time in many areas, she could be quite conservative in others. She disapproved of Countess Markievicz's habit of wearing men's trousers and tried – unsuccessfully – to make her wear a skirt over them!

St Ultan's Children's Hospital in Charlemont Street was founded in 1919 by Doctor Kathleen Lynn and Madeline Ffrench-Mullen; this was the first hospital in Ireland to cater exclusively for the needs of sick infants. The women opened the hospital with just £70 and two cots in a dilapidated building that had once been used by Lord Charlemont as a shooting gallery. Dr Lynn and her colleagues set up the hospital in an attempt to combat the high mortality rate among Dublin infants from diseases such as TB and influenza. The hospital was renowned for its innovations: it had a BCG unit and one of the first Montessori units in the world. During the early days of the hospital, milk supplies were obtained from two goats that had been donated by benefactors. One of the goats, said to be a stubborn old beast and difficult to milk, was called Lady Carson after the wife of the Ulster Unionist politician Edward Carson.

Dr Lynn carried on her work at the hospital even though she was 'on the run' from the British. She avoided capture by, in her own words, 'dressing like a lady, in my Sunday clothes and feather boa, and by walking instead of cycling.' She stood for Sinn Féin in the local elections in 1920 and was elected to Rathmines Urban District Council and later to Dublin Corporation. In 1923, she was elected to Dáil Éireann on an anti-Treaty ticket.

St Ultan's became part of the Charlemont Clinic in the 1980s.

LOBSANG RAMPA

During the course of his mysterious and intriguing life, Doctor Tuesday Lobsang Rampa, who lived in Howth for several years, devoted his time and energy to writing books on Tibetan Buddhism and the occult. But despite his exotic-sounding name, Dr Rampa was not all he appeared to be. He was eventually unmasked and revealed to be Cyril Henry Hoskins, a plumber from Devon. His cover was blown after the publication of his first book, *The Third Eye*. Rampa had walked into the office of the London publishers Secker and Warburg in 1946 and asked them to publish his life story. He arrived at the office with his head shaved and wearing the robes of a Tibetan lama, and announced himself as Doctor Tuesday Lobsang Rampa.

The Third Eye, an extraordinary book, allegedly told the story of Rampa's early life in Tibet. He claimed that he had trained to be a lama at Lhasa and that he had undergone an operation to open up a third eye in the middle of his forehead. Rampa also claimed that he had been trained to run through the air at four hundred miles an hour and that he had been schooled in the arts of crystal-gazing, aura-defining and other magical practices.

After the publication of the book, a group of Tibetan scholars became suspicious of Rampa and hired a private detective to check out his claims. The detective – Clifford Burgess – discovered that Hoskins had not only falsely assumed the persona of a Tibetan monk but that he had never set foot in Tibet. Hoskins had gained his knowledge of Tibet from books borrowed in London libraries. He had bought himself a set of lama's robes and shaved his head, and had begun to refer to himself as Doctor Kuan Suo.

When challenged with this evidence, Hoskins explained that while his outer shell was indeed that of a Devon plumber, his body had been taken over by the spirit of a Tibetan lama and that this lama was writing the books!

Hoskins' connection with Dublin began in the 1950s after an astral visit from the Dalai Lama, who told him to leave London and go to the Irish capital. In his third book, *The Rampa Story*, Hoskins relates how the lama instructed him to travel to Dublin, which he referred to as the 'green city'. Hoskins, accompanied by his wife and his telepathic Siamese cat, arrived in Dublin and rented rooms overlooking the grounds of Trinity College. Later, while writing his book *Doctor from Lhasa*, he moved to Howth, where he lived in a house overlooking Balscadden Bay.

He was very fond of the Dublin mountains and spent a great deal of his spare time driving there and enjoying the scenery. On one trip to the mountains he came across an abandoned Siamese cat. Hoskins rescued the cat and named it Mrs Fifi Greywhiskers. When he wrote a book afterwards called *Living with the Lama*, Hoskins claimed that the lama had communicated the story telepathically to him via Mrs Fifi Greywhiskers, who was clearly as gifted as his other cat! When he got fed up with driving in the Dublin mountains, Hoskins resorted to a spot of astral flying over Howth and Dublin. Returning from one nocturnal trip he complained, rather bizarrely, that seagulls had bent the rods on his aerial and that he would have to get in a local builder to fix it.

Hoskins left Ireland rather abruptly after receiving a 'savage assessment' from the Irish tax office. He said that he would have liked to stay in Ireland 'tax or no tax' but he had received another astral visit from the Dalai Lama, who instructed him to go to the 'land of the red Indians'. He went to Canada, where he continued to write his books until his death in 1981.

The Huguenot Weavers

The famous Coombe district in Dublin was at one time home to a prosperous and thriving weaving trade. The Dublin weavers were renowned for their skills in the manufacture of silk, linen and poplin. This success was mainly due to the talents of the Huguenot refugees who settled here after being driven from France by King Louis XIV during the seventeenth century.

The Huguenots were invited to come to Dublin by Dublin Corporation in 1681. Although there was a charitable motive behind this invitation, the corporation also wanted to expand manufacturing industry in the city. To this end, a collection was taken up in the city for the persecuted Huguenots and they were offered a five-year period free from taxes in an effort to encourage them to settle in Dublin.

The weavers, also known as the Guild of the Blessed Virgin Mary, built their first guild hall in 1682 in the lower Coombe. It cost the princely sum of £209. The hall was replaced by a more impressive structure in 1745. The Master of the Guild, James Digges La Touche, gave £200 towards the cost of the new building. The La Touche family had a long-standing connection with the weavers' guild and in 1767 James Digges La Touche's son John was given the freedom of the guild. Another son, Theophilus, was given the same honour in 1772. The hall was rented out to various groups for their meetings over the years and in 1797 it was leased to the Liberty Rangers for use as a guardroom and as a store for their arms and ammunition.

The weavers were quickly absorbed into the life of the city. Every three years, along with all the other guilds of the city, they were summoned by the Lord Mayor to attend the 'Riding of the Franchises' of the city.

Apprentice weavers, who had to serve a seven-year apprenticeship, were subject to a harsh disciplinary code and in 1605 a complaint recorded in the *Calendar of Ancient Records of Dublin* showed that the wearing of long hair had become popular among the apprentices. The Masters of the weavers' guild were ordered to stamp out this 'vice of long hair and other fashions' or else suffer a fine of twenty shillings. The city fathers further decreed that if any apprentice was still found to have long hair within one month of the publication of the order, the offender was to be bodily removed to the Weavers' Hall in the Coombe to have his hair cut off forcibly. Afterwards he was to be whipped by two hooded porters. The order would seem to have had the desired effect as there is no record that this particular punishment was ever carried out.

Towards the end of the eighteenth century, the Dublin weaving industry went into terminal decline. The greatest factor in this decline was the withdrawal of the 'bounties' in 1786. (The bounties were taxes on imports from England.) This was the final blow for an industry that was already reeling from the effects of industrial strife, and the Coombe – once the most prosperous locality in the city – soon became one of its greatest slums.

The weavers' guild (along with other guilds) finally collapsed in 1840 when an act of parliament was passed which allowed for the public election of members of Dublin Corporation for the first time. This superseded the practice that had been in place for centuries whereby the city guilds were entitled to fill a certain number of seats in Dublin Corporation.

LORD OF THE FLIES

Today's flush toilets and sanitary living conditions owe much to a Dubliner who made it his life's work to improve the cleanliness of the city. Sir Charles Cameron, who was born on 16 July 1830, was a scientist, journalist, art critic, historian and Dublin's chief medical officer. He was the first employee of Dublin Corporation to become a freeman of the city. He earned this honour in 1913 for his great work in reducing the mortality rate in Dublin, which was at that time the highest in Europe. As the public analyst for the city, he condemned thousands of tons of sub-standard food as unfit for human consumption. He also forced the corporation to withdraw the licence for the Clontarf oyster beds when he proved that they were responsible for an outbreak of enteric fever in the city. Another of Cameron's innovations was the design of an ambulance for fever patients, a design that was copied by health departments throughout the world.

Cameron spent most of his life campaigning on behalf of Dublin's poorer classes and in 1911 was behind a novel campaign to rid the city of houseflies. The problem was particularly acute during the summer of that year, with swarms of insects everywhere. Cameron unveiled a scheme offering three pence for every bag of dead flies presented to the cleansing depot at Marrowbone Lane. The scheme never really caught on, mainly due to the size of the paper bags supplied by the Corporation. It was estimated that it would take at least 6,000 flies to fill a bag! But the campaign was a great source of amusement to the Dublin public. One entrepreneur suggested importing the insects from abroad and selling them to the Corporation. Even 'Big Jim' Larkin got in on the act. Writing in the *Irish Worker* in September 1911, he suggested that the 'bags be opened and pinned to the middle of the clothes line . . . flies will then walk along the line from both ends and, as a result of the impact when they knock heads together, will fall senseless into the bags.'

Cameron was also the brains behind Belleek china. When on holiday at Lough Erne, he spotted porcelain clay on the estate of his friend John Caldwell-Bloomfield. Nobody believed that real china clay could be found in Fermanagh, so Cameron started a 'china war' in the local newspapers. He was vindicated when a factory opened at Belleek, providing employment to local people. Belleek china is now world-famous.

Cameron received a knighthood in 1885 in recognition of his efforts to have the poor of Dublin properly housed. Although he was a humble man, he used the title to maximum advantage to advance the cause of the poor of the city. But he later recalled that the high point of his life was on 24 February 1911, when he was made an honorary freeman of his native city. Up to that time only sixteen people had been granted this honour, including Daniel O'Connell, William Gladstone and General Grant, President of the United States.

Cameron died on 27 February 1921 at his home in Raglan Road and was buried in Mount Jerome cemetery beside his wife Lucie.

MALACHI HORAN REMEMBERS

The Tallaght of today would be virtually unrecognisable to Malachi Horan of Killinarden. Malachi was born in 1847, and his wonderful memory was not discovered until Dr George Little of the Old Dublin Society first heard of him and visited him in 1942. During the following three years, until Malachi died at the age of ninety-eight, Dr Little made extensive notes of his memories dating from Famine times right through the two world wars, the War of Independence, the Civil War and the creation of the Free State.

Malachi, who lived his whole life in a small cottage on Killinarden Hill, even published a book in 1943, at the age of ninety-six, called *Malachi Horan Remembers*. It became a best-seller and was reprinted three times. His remarkable memory gives a fascinating insight into an Ireland that has long since disappeared. The following is a description from his book of his father's attire in the nineteenth century:

He was a fine figure of a man. Anyone would have thought that, to see him on the Mass path beyond of a Sunday. When he dressed himself he would wear the felt half-tall hat which was known here as 'a nailer's chimney'. He would wear a 'trusty', or as you would call it a 'cotamore' – the name people had on it hereabout was a 'bang-up'. This was a frieze coat that reached the ankles and which had attached to it a cape on the wrists. It was heavy but very warm – a first-rate protection when driving. Beneath the coat he wore corduroy or moleskin breeches above grey stockings.

He goes on to explain that 'Mass paths' – short cuts for people going to Mass – were hated by the landlords. These were actually the forerunners of many of the rights of way in the country. In his father's time, the landlord of the Killinarden area had tried to close one, but on legal advice the locals were told to pull down every fence he put up. They also put back stepping stones in the stream time and time again, until finally they got their way. A granddaughter of the landlord, McGrane, to whom Malachi refers in the book, wrote to *The Irish Times* and the *Evening Mail* after reading his book to correct the impression that McGrane had tried to block the Mass path. It was his steward who had blocked the way, she said.

Malachi also told a fascinating tale of the time his father, Pat Horan, was accused of being an informer by the Whitefeet secret society during the time of the Land League. He was tried by a jury of his peers and 'prosecuted' by a local man, Billy Moore. After the 'hedge lawyers' argued the case, he was found innocent of the charge and told to go home. A short time later he hired the same Billy Moore to work on the farm. When Malachi queried the sense of employing a man who had wanted to shoot him, this is what his father told him: 'Let you remember Malachi, if you have an enemy and him free to harm you, contrive it that your eye is never off him. Put him, if you can, where his daily bread will depend on you. Keep him closer nor a friend. You will be safe as long as you can so keep him.'

This short space cannot do justice to the wonders of Malachi's clear memory or Dr Little's splendid work in chronicling a world gone by. Irish Folklore Commission archivist Sean Ó Súilleabháin described it as a national service in his introduction to the book. Sixty years on, it remains a national treasure.

The New Music Hall

In December 1741 George Friedrich Handel opened the doors of the music hall on Dublin's Fishamble Street and gave his first performance in the city. It wasn't the *Messiah* (yet) but it attracted an audience of 600 and he considered it a resounding success. In a letter to a friend in England he wrote: 'The nobility did me the honour to make amongst themselves a subscription for six nights, which did fill a room of six hundred persons, so that I needed not sell one single ticket at the door, and without vanity the performance was received with a general approbation.'

Handel gave another performance in the music hall three weeks later in aid of Mercer's Hospital and the Charitable Infirmary, and this too was a sell-out. For his third performance, a week later, the 'ladies and gentlemen' of Dublin were requested to order their sedan chairs and coaches to travel down through Fishamble Street towards the Liffey in order to avoid a repetition of the traffic chaos of the previous week.

The famous New Music Hall in Fishamble Street was built in 1741 by an organisation known as the Bull's Head Musical Society. Formed at the beginning of the eighteenth century, the society took its name from the Bull's Head Tavern in Fishamble Street where the members met every Friday evening. The society staged concerts at the tavern; the entrance fee for these events was one crown per head. The profits were usually donated to charity and were also used on occasion to secure the release of inmates from the city's debtors' prisons. The Bull's Head Musical Society was popular among members of the St Patrick's and Christchurch choirs. Membership of the society was discouraged by the church hierarchy and in 1741 Jonathan Swift, Dean of St Patrick's, ordered his staff to discourage choir members from patronising this 'club of fiddlers'.

The Society decided to move to a new headquarters and commissioned the architect Richard Cassels, designer of Leinster House, to build a music hall in Fishamble Street. The New Music Hall opened its doors to the public for the first time on 2 October 1741.

The first public rehearsal of the *Messiah*, in which the choirs of St Patrick's and Christchurch Cathedrals participated, took place on 8 April 1742. The *Freeman's Journal* reported that 'it gave universal satisfaction to all those present, and was allowed by the greatest judges to be the finest composition of music that was ever heard.' The *Messiah*'s first full performance took place five days later, on 13 April 1742. On that occasion, over 700 people attended the Music Hall; it was requested that ladies come without their dress hoops and gentlemen without their swords in order to make some space.

THE OLD BRIDGE

The bridge over the River Liffey linking Church Street with Bridge Street has, according to J. W. De Courcy's *The Liffey in Dublin*, 'shared fifteen names in the last thousand years.' Over the centuries it has been called: *Droichead Dubhghaill* – 'Bridge of the Dark Foreigners', Dane's Bridge, Ostman's Bridge and the Black Dane's Bridge. In medieval times the bridge was variously known as King John's Bridge, Dublin Bridge and the Friar's Bridge. This was the only bridge over the Liffey until the bridge known as the Bloody Bridge was built in the 1670s.

One of the earliest references to a bridge at the location refers to a skirmish after the Battle of Clontarf at 'the Bridge of the Dubhghaill' in which nine Norsemen were slaughtered at the head of the bridge by Tadhg O'Kelly. It was recorded a hundred and fifty years later that a Dublin city official who had been cursed by Bishop Laurence O'Toole died after a fall from the bridge.

John Gilbert recorded an ancient tale concerning the Old Bridge in his *History of the City of Dublin*. This story relates to a visit by Little John – Robin Hood's sidekick – to Dublin in 1189. According to this legend, Little John, who had been persuaded to perform feats of archery for the amusement of the citizens, 'stood on the bridge of Dublin', from where he managed to hit a target on Oxmanstown Green with an arrow. For many years afterwards the spot was known as 'Little John His Shot'.

The bridge fell down in 1385 and for the next forty years or so a ferry was used in its place. The toll rate was one farthing per person and the same for a sheep or a hog (dead or alive), while the charge for a cow, horse or side of beef was a halfpenny. During the fifteenth century the bridge was rebuilt at the request of the Dominican Order, which had a theological school at Usher's Island. Dr Thomas Burke, the Catholic bishop of Ossory, recalled in *Hibernia Dominicana* that he remembered as a boy seeing a Dominican friar standing on the bridge collecting tolls and describes a water font on the bridge from which he sprinkled the punters with holy water.

At the end of the seventeenth century, lamps were erected on the Old Bridge. This marked the beginning of a craze among the youth of Dublin that involved jumping from the top of the lamp standards into the Liffey. One of the earliest recorded 'jumpers' was the actor Charles Macklin, who is said to have performed the feat in 1705. Forty years later, the bridge was the favoured begging pitch of Patrick Corrigan, 'King of the Dublin Beggars'. Corrigan travelled to his pitch each day in a little cart drawn by a mule or his two dogs.

The old bridge began to show signs of wear and tear during the eighteenth century. When it began to attract descriptions such as a 'crazy, wretched pile of antiquity' and a 'blemish amidst so many fine pontal edifices', its days were numbered. Work on a new bridge began in 1816 and it was completed two years later. While this new bridge was under construction, the foundations of three of the earlier bridges at the site were uncovered. The new bridge was called the Whitworth Bridge in honour of Charles Earl Whitworth, Lord Lieutenant of Ireland from 1813 to 1817. The name was changed to the Dublin Bridge in 1922 and again in 1938 to Father Mathew Bridge in honour of Theobald Mathew, the Capuchin apostle of temperance.

MY BROTHER-IN-LAW ADOLF

Dublin woman Bridget Dowling was a sister-in-law of Adolf Hitler. She met Alois Hitler, the Führer's half-brother, at the 1909 Dublin Horse Show, where he was posing as a wealthy hotel owner. In reality, Alois was working as a waiter in the Shelbourne Hotel in Dublin. The smartly dressed Hitler struck up a conversation with Bridget's father, William, while they were looking at horses at the show. Seventeen-year-old Bridget immediately became interested in the handsome young Austrian and they began to meet regularly.

Bridget's family disapproved of the relationship, so the following year she and Alois eloped to London, where they married in secret. William Dowling attempted (unsuccessfully) to have Hitler charged with kidnapping. Father and daughter were reconciled a year later in Liverpool when Bridget gave birth to a son, William Patrick Hitler. In 1914 Alois abandoned his family and went to Germany to sell razor blades. The First World War kept him there for the next four years. During that time, he faked his own death and married again bigamously. He was eventually caught and prosecuted by the German authorities but was released after Bridget spoke up for him in court.

In later years Bridget and William Patrick attempted to exploit their relationship with the Führer. Bridget wrote a book entitled *My Brother-in-Law Adolf* in 1939, but it wasn't published until 1979. In it, Bridget took the credit for introducing Hitler to astrology. She also claims to have advised him to trim his moustache. Later she saw a picture of him in a newspaper and was pleased that he had taken her advice but commented that 'Adolf had gone too far'. Bridget also reveals in the book – which has been dismissed as largely a work of fiction – that Adolf Hitler himself had stayed with her, Alois and baby William at their Liverpool home for a period in 1913.

William Patrick also tried to jump on the bandwagon by attempting to blackmail Hitler. He wrote to the Führer, threatening to expose a Jewish connection in their family history. Later on, while working as a car salesman, William tried to get his uncle to use his influence to get him a better job. Hitler replied, 'I didn't become Chancellor for the benefit of my family . . . I can't have people saying I show favouritism to my family. No one is going to climb on my back.' William Patrick continued to milk the family connection for all it was worth. In 1937 he said in an interview, 'I am the only legal descendant of the Hitler family.' He then crossed his arms in a gesture that was characteristic of the tyrant and said, 'That gesture must be in the blood. I find myself doing it more and more.'

During the Second World War, William spent some time in the US navy. He toured the United States giving lectures about his famous uncle. After the war he changed his name and disappeared from public view. William 'Paddy' Hitler died in 1987, while his mother, Bridget Dowling Hitler, was last known to be living at Highgate in London during the 1950s.

The Parish Watch

Before the introduction of the Dublin Police Act in 1786, the protection of the citizens of Dublin was carried out by the parish watch. In the mid-eighteenth century, each parish in Dublin had a watch system in place. The parish watches were then under the control of the church wardens in each of the city's twenty-one parishes and consisted of around a dozen watchmen per parish. They were presided over by a parish constable who was nominated by the church warden.

The ranks of the watch were generally made up of invalids, ex-soldiers, or servants who had seen better days. These people seem to have been totally ineffective crime-fighters. They were often given positions as watchmen to prevent them from becoming burdens on the parish. The members of the watch sometimes dressed in long coats and carried a long pole with a spear on the end and a lantern. The watch patrolled only at night; their beat lasted from 11 PM to 5 AM during the summer months and from 10 PM to 6 AM in winter.

The parish watch was notoriously inefficient; corruption was rife within its ranks and they did little to prevent crime. If anything, they added considerably to the crime rate of the city. Drunkenness and absenteeism were big problems and there are numerous instances of watchmen being involved in blackmail and extortion.

An anonymous letter written to a Member of Parliament in 1765 describes the frustration of the citizens at an apparent lack of will – on the government's part – to tackle the burgeoning crime wave in the city. The letter, reprinted in the *Irish Jurist* in

1988, tells of the prevailing atmosphere of fear in the city:

> The higher sort were attacked in their carriages, plundered
> and abused, and put in fear and danger of their lives. The
> trader, after the close of day, was afraid to stir out of his
> house . . . the shopkeeper, with reluctance, kept his shop
> open: the journeyman, in dread, carried home his work,
> to receive payment due for his week's labour: old men,
> young women, servants and children were alike the prey
> of these rapacious villains.

The writer also sums up the public attitude to the parish
watch:

> Our defence against these desperadoes at present are the
> parish watches. But this guard, by woeful experience, is
> found to be feeble and insufficient . . . newspapers
> generally tell us that when the facts are committed there
> was not a watchman on his stand, or within call; so that
> nine in ten of the robbers escape the watch . . .

One of the better-organised parish watch systems was at
Blackrock. In December 1782 the Blackrock Felons' Association
was formed under the chairmanship of William Ogilvie. The
stated aim of the association was the catching and convicting
of all those involved in any type of crime in the Blackrock area.
The association was funded by some of its wealthier members,
such as the La Touche family and Viscount Ranelagh. By 1784,
the BFA had recruited two full-time constables; the sum total
of their arsenal was twelve truncheons. By the following year,
enough money had been gathered to provide them with a case
of pistols. A short time afterwards, the association decided to
build a small jail-cum-police station, and a house was rented
from William Ogilvie at one guinea a year for that purpose.

THE GOOSE PIE

The magnificent Bank of Ireland building opposite Trinity College at College Green was formerly the Irish Parliament House. The present building was erected between 1729 and 1739 and has been altered many times over the years. The site had originally been occupied by a hospital built at the end of the sixteenth century by Sir George Carey, who had intended to use it for 'poor, sick and maimed soldiers'. John Gilbert described the house as 'a large mansion with a gatehouse, a garden and plantations'. During the early part of the eighteenth century, it became the residence of Sir Arthur Chichester, until it was taken over by the Irish parliament in 1827.

The Parliament House was sometimes referred to as 'the Goose Pie' by the citizens of Dublin. This was because of its rounded roof but the nickname was also indicative of their attitude to the incompetence of the MPs who inhabited the building.

In 1759 the Parliament House was the scene of serious rioting following rumours that an Act of Union was imminent. Thousands of Dubliners laid siege to the building and several MPs were physically attacked. One MP named Rowley was stripped naked and narrowly avoided being thrown into the Liffey, while another, Sir Thomas Prendergast, was led from the building by the nose and dragged through the sewer. The rioters then took over the House of Lords, where they installed a pipe-smoking old woman on the throne. The mob erected a gallows in the building, with the intention of hanging the Master of the Rolls, Richard Rigby, who was blamed for advocating the Bill of Union. Luckily for him, he had the good fortune – or sense to be out of the city at the time. The riot was eventually put down by the military; fifteen or sixteen people were killed in the process.

When Charles Manners, Duke of Rutland and Lord Lieutenant of Ireland, died in 1787, his body lay in state in the Parliament House for several days. The duke was said to have died as a result of overindulgence at the 'splendid and numerous banquets' that he hosted while in office, but the possibility also exists that his end was hastened by numerous visits to Madame Peg Plunket's high-class bordello at Pitt Street. The walls and floors of the Parliament House were covered in black cloth for the occasion of the lying in state, and his coffin was flanked by what were then described as two lines of 'mutes', dressed in long black caps and gowns.

The Parliament House was also used on occasion as a court of law, the most high-profile case to be tried there being that of Henry Barry, the fourth Lord Santry, who was charged with the murder of a pot-boy at the Black Swan Inn in Palmerstown in 1738.

Following the Act of Union in 1801, the Parliament House became surplus to the British government's requirements and it was sold to the Bank of Ireland in 1803 for £40,000.

PEG WOFFINGTON

One of Ireland's foremost theatrical figures during the eighteenth century was Dublin-born Margaret 'Peg' Woffington (1720–60). Peg's father, John Woffington, was a poor bricklayer. The family lived in a slum at George's Court off South Great George's Street. Peg's father died when she was only five years old and Peg, her mother and her younger sister were left destitute. Peg's mother was forced to take in laundry to try and make ends meet. During those early impoverished days Peg – although only five years old – helped her mother by carrying pitchers of water from the Liffey. She also managed to make a contribution to the family finances by selling fruit and vegetables in College Green.

When Peg was about ten years old a famous French tightrope dancer called Madame Violante opened an entertainment booth at Fowne's Court. She took Peg on as a pupil and taught her to dance and sing. It wasn't long before Peg made her acting debut as Polly Peachum in a play called *The Beggar's Opera*. The play was a runaway success and launched Peg on the road to stardom, although she still had to help sell oranges to the punters before the show and during the interval.

Following the demise of Madame Violante's venture in 1734 or 1735, Peg first trod the boards at the Theatre Royal in Aungier Street, but she really made her name at the famous Smock Alley Theatre, where she often performed with the leading actors of the day, including the famous David Garrick. Peg was particularly loved by the

Dublin audiences for her performances in comedies such as *The Recruiting Officer* and *The Constant Couple*. Her performance as a man in *The Constant Couple* was her best-known role.

Peg moved to London in 1740, where her performances drew great acclaim at Drury Lane and Covent Garden. She returned to Dublin in 1751 and lived at a house in Capel Street for the next three years. During that time she was the president and only female member of the Beefsteak Club, formed by the manager of Smock Alley, Thomas Sheridan. There were similar clubs in most other theatres where the actors, along with leading literary figures and artists, dined once a week. The Beefsteak Club differed in that the membership of fifty or sixty was chiefly made up of MPs and lords. Actors and women – with the exception of Peg – were excluded from membership of the club. One member claimed that Peg was allowed to join because she had 'an understanding rarely found in females'.

In March 1754, when Peg was performing in a play called *Mahomet* at Smock Alley, the theatre was wrecked by a mob. Peg tried to remonstrate with the crowd, but to no avail. They proceeded to rip out the seats and private boxes and then attempted to set the theatre on fire. Peg left Dublin soon afterwards and returned to London, where she enjoyed even more success at Covent Garden. Her theatrical career ended in 1757 when she collapsed on stage during a performance of Shakespeare's *As You Like It*.

Peg Woffington spent the last three years of her life in retirement at her home in Teddington on the banks of the River Thames. During those last years of her life she was a reformed character and spent her time on charity work. She died on 28 March 1870 at the age of thirty-nine; her body lies in a vault in the parish church at Teddington.

POACHING IN THE PARK

One of Dublin's most beautiful amenities, the Phoenix Park, is also one of the largest enclosed urban parks in the world. It has a circumference of approximately seven miles, containing a total area of 1,752 acres. The lands where the park now stands were previously owned by the Knights Hospitaller of Kilmainham. After the dissolution of the monasteries by Henry VIII, they eventually passed into the hands of Sir Edward Fisher, who built a mansion called Phoenix House on Thomas Hill where the Magazine Fort now stands. It has been suggested by some that the park had been named after Phoenix House. F. E. Ball in his *History of the County Dublin* says that the name Phoenix was chosen for the house because of its 'commanding position and splendid outlook' over the city of Dublin and surrounding areas.

According to C. T. McCready, the name 'Phoenix' has little to do with the fabled bird that rose from the ashes. In his *Dublin Street Names* of 1892 he says that the name is a corruption of the Irish words *'fionn uisce'*, meaning 'clear water'. According to McCready, this was a reference to the *fionn uisce* spring located just outside the wall of the Viceregal Lodge (now Áras an Uachtaráin). He also says that the name 'Phoenix' became popular with the people of Dublin after 1745 when the Earl of Chesterfield, Philip Stanhope, built a pillar near the well with a large phoenix on top of it. Stanhope, who was lord lieutenant of Ireland at that time, opened up the park to the public and ordered that 'this wild and uncultivated land be ornamented for the pleasure of the citizens'.

The construction of the Phoenix Park as we know it today began in 1662 when the Duke of Ormonde decided to build a royal deer park on the site, surrounded by a stone wall. In fact, the park was often called the Deer Park in official correspondence until the late eighteenth century. The building of the wall caused a minor scandal at the time when it was discovered that the official contractor to the government, William Dodson, had used inferior materials and unskilled labour in its construction. He had built the wall so badly that it had fallen down in at least a dozen places before the construction was complete. Amazingly, the government later entered into an agreement with Dodson, who promised to maintain the walls for £100 per year. Several years later it was discovered that he had subcontracted this work out to his workmen at a cost of £30 per year, making himself a tidy profit in the process.

The park was used for many years by the Irish nobility as a hunting ground by day and it was well stocked with deer, partridge and pheasant. By night, however, it was the preserve of the poachers of Dublin, who took their share of his lordship's deer and pheasants. They also cleaned out the entire stock of partridges, which had been specially imported from Wales at great expense and inconvenience.

Dublin Zoo in the Phoenix Park opened its gates to the public 170 years ago. The zoo is believed to be the second-oldest privately owned zoo in the world. The oldest is at Regent's Park in London.

The Pigeon House

The Pigeon House at Ringsend was originally a blockhouse, used for the storage of wreckage and as a repository for tools and materials. The blockhouse was built sometime around 1760, and an employee of the Ballast Board, John Pidgeon, became caretaker there in 1761. His duties included acting as watchman over the Ballast Board's properties, and he was allowed to live in the blockhouse with his family.

At that time the cross-channel packet ships moored at the blockhouse, and Pidgeon and his wife and daughter soon established a trade providing passengers with refreshments. Because of his connection with the blockhouse, the building came to be known as Pidgeon's House, a name that exists to the present day. Pidgeon further supplemented his income by providing services to the many day-trippers visiting the South Wall at weekends. Along with his son Ned, Pidgeon would pick up visitors at Ringsend, row them down as far as the blockhouse for food and drink and then back to the village afterwards.

One night, four men tricked their way into Pidgeon's house and attacked him and his wife. Young Ned Pidgeon was badly injured in the struggle, but he managed to escape and raise the alarm. On his return he discovered that the thieves had taken everything of value from the house and had damaged the family boat beyond repair. Shortly after the incident, John and Ned were out fishing in their boat when one of their hooks snagged on something which turned out to be the body of one of the assailants. The Pidgeons later heard that the thieves had quarrelled and one of them had been killed. John Pidgeon died soon after the incident in 1786 and his son Ned died a short time later.

Pidgeon's daughters, Mary and Rachel, were left to look after themselves. Although their experience of seamanship was limited, they continued to row travellers up and down the river. One evening, following a shipwreck near Ringsend, the sisters took part in the rescue. They managed to save three people – including a father and his young son – from the cold waters of Dublin Bay. Mary eventually married the father of the child, who was a wealthy widower from Philadelphia. It is not clear what happened to Rachel at that point, but it is believed that she followed her sister to America, where she married, never to return to Ringsend.

In 1787, the Ballast Office made plans for the enlargement and refurbishment of the blockhouse. Two rooms were reserved for the Board's use and two were given to the Inspector of Works, Francis Tunstall. The other rooms were allocated to contractors working in the area and to a Mr Patrick O'Brien and his wife. The O'Briens were housekeepers to the Board. They received no wages but were allowed to carry on the selling of alcohol to the passengers, just as the Pidgeons had done before them. A few years later, the Board decided to build a larger hotel to cater for the growing number of passengers at the South Wall. This building – known as the Pidgeon House Hotel – was in place by 1795. Mrs Tunstall ran the hotel and it was renowned for its good food and hospitality. One frequent visitor described it as being 'much frequented by good fellows for gay dinners'. It remained open until 1848, when it was converted into a military fortress and garrison by the government of the day.

A Chance of Gain

During the latter part of the eighteenth century, the state lottery was a popular fund-raising method for the government of the day. Many Dubliners had a great love of gambling of all kinds and the streets of the city were packed with lottery offices. In Dame Street alone there were six offices, and there were several more in Grafton Street.

The first state-run lottery was drawn in 1780 at the Music Hall in Fishamble Street, where Handel gave the first public performance of his *Messiah*. A large mahogany wheel was placed at the entrance to the hall and the numbers were drawn by two uniformed boys from the Blue Coat School in Phoenix Park. The lottery was later transferred to an office in Capel Street, where two wheels were set up. The first wheel was used to select the numbers, while the second was spun to determine the prize to go with each number.

Although the lotteries were run and the prizes guaranteed by the government, a small group of middlemen was allowed to buy up all the tickets and sell them on for a profit. While the price of a ticket for the state lottery (approximately five pounds) was beyond the reach of the majority of the population, most lottery offices ran their own schemes based on the numbers drawn in the state lotteries. They employed a system known as 'insuring' a ticket, whereby it was possible for the poorer classes to take part in a limited form of lottery. Although the ordinary punter was precluded from winning one of the big prizes, he did have a chance of winning a smaller prize or one of the £5 tickets.

The lottery offices were usually well lit and painted in bright, gaudy colours in order to attract custom. It seems that this was an unnecessary extravagance, as crowds flocked to the offices on a daily basis in an attempt to win their fortunes.

These lotteries were the cause of untold misery and hardship amongst the poor of Dublin and many staked everything that they had to take part in the draws. Many sold or pawned their belongings, while others resorted to robbery and violence in order to get money to buy tickets. An English visitor to Dublin in 1799 was appalled at the scenes he witnessed at these offices: 'In these shops are the most ragged objects (of which Dublin perhaps contains more than any other city in Europe) staking their daily bread on a chance of gain.' A Dublin Corporation report ten years earlier condemned the evils of the lottery offices: 'It hath induced many servants to pilfer and steal in order to pursue a chance that seems to elude all pursuit.' The report also blamed the lotteries for making 'the honest and industrious, corrupt and idle, for during the drawing of the lottery, their minds are too much interested and agitated to attend to their respective employments.'

In 1785, a young postal worker, Alex McLivery, was arrested and charged with stealing lottery tickets with a view to selling them on. He was the first person to be charged under the provisions of the harsh Postal Act of 1784. McLivery was found guilty of the crime and was publicly hanged outside Newgate Prison in March 1786.

The government came under increasing pressure from religious and charitable bodies to regulate the lotteries and in 1793 the practice of 'insuring' tickets was outlawed. Tighter controls were introduced on the lottery offices, making it more difficult for people to bet, and interest in the lotteries declined as a result.

GHOSTS AND TREMORS

Rathfarnham Castle was built over four hundred years ago by the Archbishop of Dublin, Adam Loftus. Loftus leased the lands in 1582 and the construction of the castle was complete by 1585. A contemporary scribe described the castle as 'an edifice of such magnificence as would for all time be a monument to the greatness and grandeur of its builder.'

Loftus was reputed to have had twenty children during his lifetime. His eldest son, Dudley Loftus, inherited Rathfarnham on his father's death in 1605. During the rebellion of 1641, the Loftus family took precautions to prevent the castle falling into the hands of the rebels. In Easter week of that year, the rebels captured Henry Butterfield of Rathfarnham and hanged him at Powerscourt. Seven years later, the castle was garrisoned by the Parliamentarian army. Five hundred Royalists stormed and captured the garrison shortly before the Battle of Rathmines with no loss of life on either side.

In 1691, Adam Loftus was killed at the Siege of Limerick when he was hit by a stray cannon ball. Rathfarnham Castle then passed into the hands of the Wharton family, who managed to run the estate into the ground in a very short time. The next owner of the castle was William 'Speaker' Connolly, who bought it and the lands adjoining for £62,000. In 1767, the castle once more reverted to the Loftus family when it was bought by the Earl of Ely, Nicholas Loftus. In 1852, it was sold to the Blackburn family and in 1913 it was bought by the Jesuits.

It seems that every castle must have its own ghost story and Rathfarnham is no exception to this. For many years, it was said that Rathfarnham was haunted by the ghost of a dog. During the harsh winter of 1841, the pond at the castle had frozen over. A young man was skating across the pond when the ice cracked and he disappeared below the surface. His dog – a retriever – jumped in after him and both were drowned. For many years afterwards it was reported that the ghost of the dog was seen regularly in and around the grounds of the castle. There was also a haunted room at the top of the north-east tower. Local tradition has it that the skeleton of a woman sitting in a chair was discovered behind false panelling in the room.

A seismographic observatory was used by the Jesuits at Rathfarnham Castle until 1961. A seismograph is used to measure earthquakes and earth tremors. Over the years the Jesuits made a large contribution to seismographic research and they had a large network of observatories throughout the world. In fact, seismography has often been referred to as 'the Jesuit science'.

William J. O'Leary installed the first Irish seismograph at Mungret College in Limerick in 1908 and it was transferred to Rathfarnham in 1916. O'Leary designed and built the machine himself. The main difference between Father O'Leary's seismograph and the standard machines was in the weight of the pendulum. His pendulum weighed nearly two tons, while the standard Milne-Shaw seismograph only required a weighting of one and a half pounds.

THE DEVIL'S MILL

The picturesque Luttrellstown Castle and demesne near Castleknock was for many centuries the home of the Luttrell family. The first Luttrell to come to Ireland was Geoffrey Luttrell, who was sent to Ireland by his friend King John in 1204 to act as a mediator in disputes between the justiciary and the Anglo-Norman Lords in Ireland. He returned to Ireland in 1210 when he accompanied King John on his expedition to this country.

Thomas Luttrell, who lived at Luttrellstown at the end of the fifteenth century, was once Chief Justice of the Common Pleas. This Luttrell's existence rarely took him outside the walls of the Pale and he regarded the Irish natives living outside the walls as foreigners. He urged his fellow Palesmen to take action against the Gaelic marauders in the Wicklow mountains and warned them of the dangers of employing them as soldiers. He also recommended that the Palesmen dress in the English manner and gain proficiency in the use of the longbow. He proposed a ban on Englishmen returning to their own country and advocated the expulsion of Irish bards and musicians.

The most infamous of all the Luttrells was the traitor to the Jacobite cause, Colonel Henry Luttrell. Luttrell earned the opprobrium of Irish Catholics after his defection from the army of King James II to the Williamite forces following the Siege of Limerick. He brought his entire regiment with him and later received a pension of £500 a year from William III. On the night of 3 November 1717, Henry Luttrell was being carried in a sedan chair from a coffee house on Cork Hill to his city residence in Stafford Street when an unknown assassin shot him dead. Despite the offer of a large reward from the government, the perpetrator was never caught. The following rhyme was typical of the sentiment prevailing against Henry Luttrell:

> If Heaven be pleased when mortals cease to sin,
> And Hell be pleased when villains enter in,
> If earth be pleased when it entombs a knave,
> All must be pleased – now Luttrell's in his grave.

The legend of the devil's mill on the Lutrellstown estate is connected with Henry Luttrell. The story goes that Henry managed to hoodwink the devil and escaped with his life, having entered into a pact with the devil. He agreed to build the mill, which was said to have been constructed in a single night. After the ill-fated rebellion of 1798 had been suppressed, Luttrell's grave at Clonsilla churchyard was broken open and his skull was smashed to pieces. This was probably as a direct result of the part played by Henry Luttrell's grandson Lord Carhampton in putting down the rebellion.

A seventeenth-century survey of the Barony of Castleknock leaves us with some idea of how Luttrellstown looked at that time. It was described as 'a great mansion house with twelve chimneys, surrounded by offices, and having near it a malt house, a barn and two stables.' In addition, there were three orchards, pleasure gardens and two stone quarries. The estate included two mills and a salmon weir on the Liffey.

THE DUBLIN LYING-IN HOSPITAL

The Rotunda Hospital in Parnell Square (or the Dublin Lying-in Hospital, as it was originally known) was established in 1745 by the surgeon Bartholomew Mosse, son of a Maryborough (Portlaoise) clergyman. Mosse settled in Dublin in 1742 and obtained a licence in midwifery. He opened his first hospital in George's Lane (South Great George's Street) in 1745 to alleviate the atrocious conditions then experienced by expectant mothers in the poorer sections of Dublin. One observer described the conditions facing these women:

> The misery of the poor women of the city of Dublin at the time of their lying-in would scarcely be conceived by anyone who had not been an eyewitness of their wretched circumstances; that their lodgings were generally in cold garrets, open to every wind, or in damp cellars, subject to floods from excessive rains . . . By which hundreds perished with their little infants.

Mosse opened his little hospital with only ten beds on 15 March 1745, and during the first year of the hospital's existence, it was recorded that 209 women were admitted and 190 babies delivered. The lying-in hospital was the first of its kind, not only in Ireland but in Britain. Mosse realised at an early stage that his small premises at George's Lane would not be adequate to meet the demands of a large city like Dublin. In 1748 he obtained a lease on four acres of land to the north of Sackville Street known as the 'Barley

Fields' and engaged his friend, the famous German architect Richard Cassels, to build the new hospital. Cassels based his design for the new hospital on his earlier design for Leinster House in order to save Mosse some of his hard-earned funds for the actual running of the hospital, which was largely dependent on charity.

Mosse raised funds for the hospital by a range of schemes. He established several lotteries and laid on various concerts and performances. He also had the grounds of the hospital laid out as pleasure gardens and charged an entry fee of sixpence. The pleasure gardens contained gravel walks, a bowling green and musical entertainment at the weekends. Despite all Mosse's innovations, he was still in financial trouble right from the founding of the new hospital. On the day that the foundation stone was laid in 1751, Mosse claimed that he needed at least £20,000 to complete the project. The hospital finally opened on 8 December 1757, with Mosse as its first Master.

The famous Round Room, from which the Rotunda takes its name, did not exist until after Mosse's death in 1759. It was built in 1764 to a design by Richard Ensor, a pupil of Cassels'. This design was added to and extended several time over the years and includes features by Richard Johnson and James Gandon. In 1784, Johnson was the designer of the New Assembly Rooms, which have been home to the Gate Theatre since 1929.

The Rotunda was on the verge of bankruptcy in 1785 when it was saved by an act of parliament. The act granted to the hospital the proceeds from a tax on the sedan chairs of the city. The relief from this tax was short-lived, however, as the number of sedan chairs dwindled rapidly following the Act of Union in 1801.

The Royal Hibernian Military School

A pamphlet written in 1721 gave details of a charity school set up in the Stoneybatter area in 1705 by a group of 'pious ladies'. The school, catering for twenty-five girls, taught them the 'three Rs' and 'instructed them in the ways of the Established Church'. When they had reached a sufficiently high standard, the girls were placed in trades or other suitable services.

Sixty years later, a Reverend Carr donated £100 towards the setting up of a similar charity for young boys in the area. A report in the *Freeman's Journal* of 19 February 1765 indicated that the governors of this school found themselves snowed under with applications, as in the parish of St Paul at that time there appeared to be 'above four hundred boys, all orphans, or destitute children of soldiers who had either died or were killed or absent in foreign parts in the service of the Crown'.

The Dublin Guild of Carpenters gave the governors the use of part of their premises at Oxmanstown Green for the school. The governors took in twenty boys and pledged not only to educate and clothe them, but to feed them and give them a roof over their heads until they reached an age when they could fend for themselves. By the end of April 1765, the school was catering for forty boys, all children of British soldiers. Plans were made to admit an equal number of girls and the governors set out to find a larger premises for the project.

The government of the day allocated three acres in the Phoenix Park for the project and an annual grant of £1,000.

The building, designed by the architect Francis Johnston, was completed in April 1768 and forty children were admitted to the new Royal Hibernian Military School.

The classes were set up along the lines of army companies and the boys carried out drilling and other military exercises to the beat of a drum. Admission to the school was restricted to children aged between seven and twelve and priority was given to children whose fathers had died on military service overseas. As might be expected from an institution run under military auspices, a strict regime was enforced. The boys and girls had to rise from their beds at 6 AM during the summer months and at 7.30 in winter. The next hour was devoted to personal grooming, followed by prayers and inspection. Next came breakfast, which typically consisted of one-third of a pound of bread and a pint of milk. Breakfast, like all other meals, was eaten in silence. A typical dinner consisted of one pint of ox-head soup along with one and a half pounds of potatoes per child.

In addition to their lessons, children were expected to work for their keep. The boys worked on the nineteen-acre farm attached to the school until they reached fourteen years of age, when they were usually sent out as apprentices to the various trades. Girls, who were taught knitting and sewing, generally found employment in the clothing trade.

The Royal Hibernian Military School closed its doors in September 1922 when the British administration withdrew from Dublin. The boys were transferred to barracks at Somerset and Dover. The buildings were taken over by the Free State army in December 1922. Today they are still in use as St Mary's Hospital for geriatric care.

THE CONNIVING HOUSE

Scallet Hill, Scald Hill, Scarlet Hill and Brickfield Town. Over the centuries, these were all names that described the present-day Dublin 4 suburb of Sandymount. Until the sixteenth century, it was mainly marshland and there was an extensive rabbit warren in the driest part of the area. The lands were originally owned by the Norman Richard St De Olof, who was also the owner of Simmonscourt. According to Francis Ball, the lands then passed through the hands of the Bagods, the Fitzwilliams, the Priory of the Holy Trinity and finally back into the possession of the Fitzwilliams of Merrion.

When extensive improvements to the fabric of the city were carried out in the eighteenth century, there was a great demand for building materials and it was discovered that the clay at Scallet Hill was highly suited to the manufacture of bricks. The district soon came to be known as 'Lord Merrion's Brickfields'. A new village was built to accommodate the workforce and this came to be known as Brickfield Town or Bricktown.

There are many references during that period to a tavern in Brickfield Town called the Conniving House. The proprietor of the establishment was Johnny Macklean and it was well known for its seafood and ale. Thomas Amory in his *Life of John Buncle* (1725) described the tavern as a 'delightful place of a summer's evening. Many a delightful evening have I passed in this pretty thatched house with the famous Larry Grogan, who played on the bagpipes extreme well; dear Jack Lattin matchless on the fiddle, and the most agreeable of companions . . . '

At the close of the eighteenth century, Lord Fitzwilliam built a protective wall along the coastline stretching from Merrion to Brickfields in order to safeguard his property from the ravages of the sea. From this point onwards the area started to develop as a retreat for the well-heeled citizens of Dublin and the name of the area was changed to Sandymount. After all, who'd want to build a villa in a place called Brickfield?

Throughout the nineteenth century Sandymount was described as having a fine sandy beach and was popular for sea-bathing. Lewis's *Topographical Dictionary* in 1837 described the village:

> The village is very pretty and contains many good houses forming a square, in the centre of which is an ornamental grass-plot surrounded by iron railings: there are numerous pretty villas on the strand, for the convenience of summer visitors, whence a new road to Merrion has lately been made along the shore.

Lewis also refers to the Sisters of Charity, who had moved to Sandymount in 1831. The founder of the Irish Sisters of Charity, Mother Mary Aikenhead, wrote a letter to the Poor Law commissioners in December 1833, in which she painted a dismal picture of the sufferings and deprivations of the poor of Irishtown and Ringsend during 1832 and 1833, precipitated by disease. During the course of the summer of 1833, the *cholera morbus* had broken out in Ringsend, Irishtown, Ballsbridge and Sandymount and had ripped through the community for five weeks with great ferocity. The nuns found many people dying, without even the means of getting a drink of clean water. There were numerous instances of heartbreaking misery. Many people were reduced to the edge of existence by the lack of nourishing food. More had pawned their few meagre possessions for a few pence in order to buy something to eat. There were no medical facilities until the Sisters of Charity, aided by subscriptions from Lord Anglesea and the Hon. Sidney Herbert, opened a small hospital at Irishtown. It contained twelve beds, which were constantly full until the epidemic had ended. The Sisters were also able to provide care and medicine to a hundred outpatients.

THE OLD DWELLING PLACE

The name of Santry comes from the Irish *Seantrabh* or *Sean Triabh*, which means the 'old tribe' or the 'old dwelling place'. Who exactly this 'old tribe' were or who dwelt there, we do not know. There is some archaeological evidence for pre-historic activity in the Santry area but very little is known about its history until the coming of the Normans in the twelfth century.

After the invasion, the lands at Santry were granted to the Norman knight Adam de Phepoe, whose ancestors remained there until the mid-fifteenth century. In the sixteenth century the barony passed through several hands until it came into the possession of the Dublin-based Barry family.

The Civil Survey of 1654 describes Santry as containing 'a dwelling house of stone with a barne and an old stable, thacht, ye walls of a house and a garden and two orchards. Also a small slated house with six thacht Cabbins valued by ye jury at 300li. Also ye parish church of Santry.'

In 1738, Henry Barry, the fourth Lord Santry, was tried and sentenced to death for the murder of a pot-boy at the Black Swan Inn in Palmerstown. After a day spent drinking at the bar, Barry stabbed the unfortunate pot-boy – Laughlin Murphy – to death. Barry managed to avoid the gallows after his uncle, Compton Domville, allegedly threatened to cut off the city's water supply. The River Dodder flowed through his estate at Templeogue and he declared he would divert its flow if his nephew wasn't reprieved. Barry was eventually spared on the understanding that he must leave the country.

He spent many years travelling throughout Europe until his death in 1751.

Another member of the Domville family, Charles, was Lord of Santry in 1864. Charles liked to let his workers know who was boss and on 18 May of that year he issued precise instructions about how he expected his employees to behave. He forbade his workers to smoke on his property, and conversation was only allowed between employees if it was related to the job in hand. He also demanded that a strict dress code be adhered to on his estate and is quoted as saying, 'I require every labourer to keep his clothes clean and well mended and to wear laced boots, leather gaiters to his knee, corduroy breeches and waistcoat, necktie and smock frock with a black felt hat.'

In addition, Domville expected his employees to keep their cottages and surroundings tidy and to 'make any minor repairs necessary'. He finished his edict by effectively imposing a curfew on his workers. He ordered that no worker on the estate was to 'leave home without permission, as each man is liable to be called in at night, in case of fire etc.'

Santry was once one of the most dangerous areas in the city, the scene of many mail-coach robberies throughout the seventeenth and eighteenth centuries, several of which are documented in Weston St John Joyce's *The Neighbourhood of Dublin*. Joyce relates the tale of the hijacking of the Dublin–Drogheda mail coach on 17 September 1773 at Santry. The coach was held up by two young highwaymen, who relieved the passengers of all their cash and valuables. Before fleeing with their ill-gotten gains, they took pity on one of their victims who was a priest, and returned his purse. Twenty-five years later, during the rebellion of 1798, the north mail coach was hijacked by rebels at Santry. On that occasion, Joyce tells us, the passengers were robbed of property to the value of 'between £300 and £400, including all the arms which the passengers and guard had with them for their protection'.

The Palace of St Sepulchre

The Palace of St Sepulchre was, for a period of about 600 years, the residence of the Protestant archbishops of Dublin. It was built on the site where Kevin Street garda station now stands. When the first Norman archbishop of Dublin, John Comyn, decided to build his church, St Patrick's, outside the walls of the old city on the island of the River Poddle, he also found it necessary to construct a house nearby for the use of the clergymen associated with the church. Comyn raised St Patrick's to the rank of a collegiate church and installed a 'college of clerics of approved life and learning' at St Sepulchre's.

During those times, archbishops had an even greater influence on civil matters than they do today, and the bishop of the Liberty of St Sepulchre was no different. It was within the bishop's gift to make and implement his own laws within the manor, including the right to hold courts and the power to implement the death penalty. Prisoners sentenced to death by the bishops were taken for execution to the bishops' gallows at Harold's Cross Green on the boundary of the parish.

There are few descriptions remaining of the Palace of St Sepulchre, but in 1326 it was obviously in a fairly run-down condition. The buildings were described as 'a store hall, badly roofed with shingles and weave, a chamber annexed to the said hall, a kitchen, a chapel badly roofed, valued at nothing because nothing can be received from them, but they need much repair. And there was a certain prison, now broken and thrown to the ground.'

Two hundred and fifty years later, the palace appears to have undergone extensive refurbishment, as it was described by Richard Stanihurst in the 1570s as being 'well pleasantlie sited as gloriously builded.' In his *Description and History of Ireland,* Stanihurst also related that many Dubliners were of the opinion that the most beautiful part of the building was deliberately set on fire by one of the archbishops. This was in the days before the building of the Viceregal Lodge in the Phoenix Park, and the accommodation at Dublin Castle was not satisfactory either. The irate archbishop was said to be so fed up with providing hospitality for the constant stream of royal visitors to the Palace that he burned down the guest rooms in exasperation!

Edward VI reduced the status of St Patrick's to that of a parish church, and the palace was given to the Lord Deputy of Ireland. The Archbishop was forced to move to the Deanery house of St Patrick's Cathedral. This arrangement proved to be a short-term measure, as the bishop moved back into the palace immediately after Edward's death.

Archbishop Narcissus Marsh, Archbishop of Dublin, lamented the lack of a library at the palace in a letter written to a friend in 1700. He said that although St Sepulchre's 'may well be called a palace for the stateliness of all the public rooms of reception, it has no chapel or library belonging to it, or any convenient room to hold an ordinary study of books, so that mine lies dispersed in three distant rooms.' Marsh engaged the architect of the Royal Hospital in Kilmainham – William Robinson – to design the now-famous Marsh's Library beside St Patrick's Cathedral.

When the Archbishop of Dublin moved to a new residence in the more fashionable Stephen's Green, the old palace was converted for use as a police barracks. All that now remains of the original structure is a vault and a small window dating from 500 years ago.

THE MAGNIFICENT SHERIDANS

The Sheridans originally came from County Longford, where they were *erenaghs* (hereditary churchwardens) of Granard. Later they moved to neighbouring County Cavan and became supporters of the ruling O'Reillys. To this day, the name Sheridan is most common in Cavan. Little else is known about the name except that it is derived from a first name, Sirideain.

Every famous Sheridan in Irish history seems to have been involved in some way with literature. The most famous of these was Richard Brinsley Sheridan (1751–1816), orator and playwright. He was born at Dorset Street in Dublin and was the son of another famous author, Thomas Sheridan, and his wife, the novelist Frances Chamberlain. He received his early education at Samuel Whyte's academy in Grafton Street, where a schoolmaster described him as 'a most incorrigible dunce'. In 1771 he fell in love and eloped with a beautiful young musician, Elizabeth Linley of Bath.

They went to live in London and the young Sheridan turned his hand to writing plays. His first effort, *The Rivals*, was produced at Covent Garden in 1775 and was a resounding success. The next year, Sheridan bought himself a share in Drury Lane Theatre for £35,000. Two years later he bought the remaining share for £45,000. He wrote several other plays, the most popular being *The School for Scandal* and *The Critic*.

In 1780, Sheridan turned his talents to the political stage and was elected MP for Stafford. He was renowned in the House of Commons for his brilliant oratory and he sat in parliament for thirty-two years. In 1809, Drury Lane was destroyed by fire and Sheridan lost his main source of income. He took to drinking heavily and his debts accumulated. His last years were spent in poverty and he died on 7 July 1816 with the bailiffs in possession of his home.

Another famous member of this literary family was the novelist and journalist Joseph Sheridan Le Fanu, who was a grand-nephew of Richard Brinsley. He was born in 1814 at 45 Dominick Street. He was educated privately by his father during his early years and later studied law at Trinity College. Le Fanu is mainly remembered for his immensely popular novels with supernatural themes, such as *Through a Glass Darkly* and *The House by the Churchyard*, set in Chapelizod. Le Fanu spent the last twenty years of his life residing at 18 (now 70) Merrion Square. He died in 1873 at the age of fifty-nine and was buried in Mount Jerome cemetery in Harold's Cross.

One Sheridan who made an impact on the international stage was General Philip Henry Sheridan (1831–88), born on 6 March 1831 at Killinkeere, County Cavan. He went to the United States as a child and was educated at West Point Military Academy from 1848 to 1853. During the American Civil War he fought on the Union side and rose through the ranks to the position of Major General. He orchestrated a brilliant campaign at the decisive battle in Shenandoah Valley. After the war, he became military governor of Texas and Louisiana. Sheridan was also heavily involved in the campaigns against the American Indians and it was during the 1868 war against the Cheyenne and Comanche tribes that he is said to have coined the infamous line, 'the only good Indian is a dead Indian'. In fact, the story was that a Comanche chief, Tosawi, brought his braves to Sheridan to offer his unconditional surrender. When he was introduced to Sheridan, he smiled and said in broken English, 'Tosawi, good Indian.' Sheridan's reply to Tosawi was, 'The only good Indians I ever saw were dead.'

The Turkish Bathhouse

Sir Jonah Barrington, in his *Recollections* of life in late-eighteenth-century Dublin, records the arrival in the city of a Turkish refugee who called himself Doctor Achmet Borumbad. He was a large man with a black beard and moustache and was always attired in traditional Turkish dress. Doctor Borumbad's appearance created quite a stir on the streets of Dublin and on his travels throughout the city he usually attracted large crowds of boys in his wake. Barrington described him as 'The first Turk who had ever walked the streets of Dublin in his native costume.'

Borumbad somehow managed to persuade a number of influential members of the medical profession and several prominent members of the Irish House of Commons to provide funding for a Turkish bathhouse at Bachelors Walk. Borumbad's procedure consisted of hot and cold sea-water baths. The cold pool was connected to the Liffey and the water was changed daily at high tide. Time and time again the good doctor ran out of money and on each occasion he returned to parliament to obtain further funding for the scheme. He was never refused until an incident occurred at his premises that ultimately led to his downfall.

In preparation for his visits to parliament to look for funding, it had been the Turk's practice to hold lavish banquets at the baths for his MP friends. During what proved to be the last banquet ever held there, Borumbad hosted a group of about thirty MPs. As the night progressed and the wine flowed, things began to get out of hand and one of the older MPs, Sir John Hamilton, decided to leave. He opened the wrong door on his way out and fell into the vast, cold salt-water bath. He was soon joined in the bath by eighteen other MPs who fell in while attempting to stop him from leaving.

Worse humiliation was to follow: after the Turk and his attendants had rescued the half-frozen and bedraggled members from the pool, the only spare clothing to be found on the premises was of the traditional Turkish variety, and the MPs were forced to travel home in sedan chairs, dressed in highly colourful robes.

In the meantime, the good doctor had fallen in love with a Miss Hartigan, sister of a respectable Dublin surgeon. Although she was initially attracted to Achmet's Oriental looks and whiskers, Miss Hartigan refused to have anything further to do with him until he shaved off his beard and converted to Christianity. By that time, the doctor's fortunes had taken a serious reversal. After the incident at his premises on Bachelors Walk, he had fallen out of favour with his MP friends and they had refused to advance him any more cash for his ventures. Borumbad had to do something quickly and he saw Miss Hartigan, 'a woman of means', as an ideal ticket to help him escape from his financial difficulties. Achmet Borumbad's true identity only came to light when he decided to come clean with Miss Hartigan. He shaved off his beard, got rid of the Turkish robes and revealed that, far from being a Turk, he was actually Paddy Joyce from Kilkenny. 'As good a Christian as the archbishop,' he said. 'The divil a Turk, any more than yourself, sweet angel.' Joyce had apparently hit on the idea for the Turkish-baths scam while visiting Turkey some years earlier.

ST PATRICK'S ON THE ISLAND

St Patrick's Cathedral, which stands two decent stone's-throws away from Christchurch, is believed to be located on the site of an earlier church dedicated to St Patrick. A small wooden church was built on the site and it was known as 'St Patrick's *in insula*' or 'St Patrick's on the island' because it was built on an island on the River Poddle, which still flows beneath the cathedral today. Legend suggests that the saint performed baptisms at a holy well where the park is now situated, beside the cathedral. This well was unearthed during renovations at St Patrick's in 1901, and the decorated granite lid that covered it is now on display inside the cathedral.

The present structure of the church originated during the early years of Norman rule. The first Norman bishop of Dublin, John Comyn, had the old church of St Patrick rebuilt in rough-hewn stone in a cruciform shape, and 810 years ago, on 17 March 1192, the new church was dedicated to 'God, Our Blessed Lady Mary and St Patrick'. Comyn died in 1212 and his successor, Henry of London, had the church raised to the status of a cathedral in 1216. Before his death in 1228, Henry instigated a major redesign of the cathedral and this work was not finished until 1254. The building of the Lady Chapel was completed by 1270.

When Edward de Bruce attacked the city in 1316, the citizens set fire to the cathedral rather than allow the Scots to use it as a base for attacking the city. Serious damage was done to the tower and bells of the cathedral during an accidental fire in 1362; the blaze was attributed to 'the negligence of John the Sexton'. The tower was replaced in 1370 by Archbishop Thomas Minot, although the spire that crowns it was not added until over 400 years later.

In consequence of its close proximity to the River Poddle, the cathedral suffered from serious flooding during the seventeenth and eighteenth century. In 1687, when the rest of the city was under several feet of water, the cathedral was said to be flooded to a level 'above the desks'.

An unusual feature of the cathedral is the 'door of reconciliation' now located in the western nave. This curious feature has its origins in a skirmish that took place in St Patrick's between the Earl of Kildare and the Earl of Ormonde in 1492. Ormonde was forced to flee to the chapterhouse and emerged only after Fitzgerald cut a hole in the chapterhouse door so that they could shake hands. Some writers have suggested that this incident led to the coining of the phrase 'chancing your arm', as Ormonde initially refused to put his hand through the hole, fearing that it would be hacked off with a sword.

No description of St Patrick's Cathedral would be complete without a mention of Dean Jonathan Swift, renowned for his wit and biting satire. He was the author of *Gulliver's Travels* and political works such as his *Drapier's Letters*. He was appointed Dean of St Patrick's in 1713 and served in that position for the next thirty-two years. Swift died in 1745, and when his death was announced thousands made their way to his house to pay their last respects. According to Swift's godson Thomas Sheridan, the crowd was so anxious to obtain souvenirs of the late dean that they bribed servants to snip off locks of his hair to be kept as relics. 'In less than an hour,' said Sheridan, 'his venerable head was entirely stripped of all its silver ornaments, so that not a hair remained.'

THE DUBLIN AND BLESSINGTON STEAM TRAMWAY

On Saturday 4 August 1888, the *Wicklow Newsletter* reported the opening of the Dublin and Blessington Steam Tramway. The inaugural journey had taken place three days earlier on 1 August and took one and a half hours to complete. The first tram left Terenure at 8.45 AM, calling at Templeogue and Tallaght. It then continued on its way to the Embankment, Crooksling and Brittas, among other stops, before reaching Blessington at 10.20 AM.

About eight years earlier there had been a proposal to run a light railway from St Patrick's Cathedral to Blessington under the power of steam, but the plan was scuppered by Dublin Corporation, who refused to allow steam power to be used within its jurisdiction. In 1887 the Dublin and Blessington Steam Tramway Company was given the go-ahead from the British government to build a tramline along the fifteen-mile route from Terenure to Blessington. The service was connected to the centre of Dublin by the horse-drawn trams of the Dublin Tramway Company.

The company had initially intended to extend the line as far as Poulaphouca but this didn't happen until 1895, when an offshoot company – the Blessington and Poulaphouca Steam Tramway Company – was formed. During the interim period, day-trippers were carried between Blessington and Poulaphouca by a long car pulled by two horses. It was the board of this company that made an unusual decision at its AGM in 1910, resolving: 'the staff shall be given ten years to learn Irish. That all future employees must have knowledge of the Irish language, otherwise they would not be employed.' It was also resolved that 'all official business be transacted in the above tongue, and not the barbarous tongue of the Saxon.'

The steam trams were popular with day-trippers during the summer months, and on bank holidays they were packed to capacity. The demand was so heavy during the years of the First World War that it inspired a verse from an unnamed rhymer, which commenced with the lines:

> The Battle of Ypres was only a sham
> Compared to the rush for the Blessington tram

The tramline was the scene of many accidents over the years. Soon after its opening, a woman was killed in Templeogue. This poor woman's number was surely up, as she had earlier survived an accident at Terenure, when she was run over by a horse and cart! In the first part of his autobiography, *Dublin Made Me*, Todd Andrews details the frequent fatalities that occurred on the tramline in the vicinity of Terenure and Templeogue. 'The line between Terenure and Blessington was said to be the longest graveyard in the world because of the number of plaques and crosses commemorating the various fatalities, nearly all attributable to drink.' He also tells of his fearful and morbid curiosity to see the blanket-covered corpses in the waiting room in the terminus at Terenure.

The Dublin and Blessington steam tram made its final journey on New Year's Eve in 1932. On the final leg of the return journey from Tallaght to the Templeogue depot, the tram was full to capacity and crowds lined the route to witness the close of a colourful chapter in the history of Dublin transport.

'THE KING OF SPAINE'S DAUGHTER'

That great Irish institution – the public house – was as (if not more) popular in medieval Dublin as it is today. During the seventeenth century, a Gaelic priest described Dublin in a letter as 'the city of the wine-flasks', while another writer claimed that there were 1,180 alehouses and ninety-one breweries within the confines of the city. One hundred years later, the number of alehouses had risen – according to Dr John Rutty – to 2,000. In addition, there were 1,200 brandy shops (off-licences) and 300 taverns.

During the reign of Elizabeth I, an English clerk, quoted in John Gilbert's *History of the City of Dublin*, spoke of the availability of French and Spanish wines in Dublin, which were sold by the pint and quart. He commented that 'when the native Irish come to any market towne to sell a cow or a horse, they never returne home till they have drunke the price in Spanish wine (which they call the King of Spaine's daughter), or in Irish Usqueboagh.'

Winetavern Street, or Vicus Tabernarioum Vini as it was known from early medieval times, was once teeming with drinking establishments. Some of the taverns seen there in the seventeenth century were the Black Boy Cellar, the Spread Eagle and the Golden Dragon. Barnaby Rich, in a tirade against tavern-keepers in 1624, claimed that most of the wealth of Dublin came through the sale of drink. 'There are,' he said, 'whole streates of tavernes, and it is as rare a thing to finde a house in Dubline without a tavern, as to find a tavern without a strumpet.' Rich, obviously embittered by a 'bad pint' experience in Dublin, ends his outburst with a colourful description of the local brew: 'The very remembrance of that hogges wash which they used to sell . . . is able to distemper any man's braines, and as it is neither good nor wholesome, so it is unfit for any mans drinking, but for common drunkards.'

In 1633, the Lord Deputy of Ireland took action to remove the alehouses and tobacco shops that flourished in the vaults underneath Christchurch Cathedral. He wrote to the archbishop of Canterbury complaining that the natives were 'pouring either in or out their drink offerings and incense, whilst we above are serving the high God.' Another writer of that period recounted his fears that the 'Popish recusants' in their beer- and wine-tippling rooms beneath the cathedral might poison the assembled churchgoers above with their alcoholic fumes.

One of the most fashionable taverns of the eighteenth century was the Phoenix tavern in Werburgh Street. It was heavily frequented by members of the Irish House of Commons and political leaders of all hues. In 1752, it was the headquarters of the Grand Lodge of Freemasons and six years later it was used by groups such as the Hibernian Society and the Friendly Florists Society. In 1771, the 'Constitutional Society' held debates at the Phoenix. The cover charge of one shilling entitled the guests to 'moderate' quantities of wine.

DOING A RUNNER

One hundred and sixty years ago, a Dublin judge – Frank Porter – had a reputation for being unusually severe with any 'drink driving' cases that appeared in his court. In the 1840s a Rathfarnham cabman appeared before him charged with being drunk and incapable while in charge of his horse and carriage. The case caused a great dilemma for the judge, who recognised the cabman as the man who had once saved him from drowning while he was swimming at a quarry in Kimmage. The judge went ahead and convicted his saviour, and revoked his licence. Judge Porter mentioned the drowning incident to the public gallery, citing it as proof of his tough stance on drink driving. The judge was definitely playing to the gallery on that occasion, for on his way home that evening he dropped into the carriage office and arranged with his good friend Colonel Browne, the Police Commissioner, to have a new licence given to the driver.

Another case involving a cabman came before the courts in 1854. One day, the jarvey in question was waiting for a fare at Islandbridge Barracks. A captain of the 'Scots Greys' regiment was amusing himself with a small handgun. He aimed the gun at the cabman and shot him twice, wounding him slightly in the back and leg. The cabman, fearing for his life, applied the whip liberally to his horse's back and managed to drive himself to the Meath Hospital, where he had the pellets extracted from his leg. When the case came before the court, the judge expressed the opinion that the assault had been carried out 'more in a spirit of foolish fun than in any wish to injure the complainant' and he suggested that if the captain should offer compensation to the cabman, the matter would end there and then. The captain – a man of means – offered the cabman £100 for his troubles, which he accepted with enthusiasm. Turning to the judge, the cabman said: 'The business is settled, yer worship, and I can only say that when I was hit, although it gave me a great start, I felt satisfied that it was a *rale gintleman* that shot me.' The money proved to be the undoing of the cabman, as he drank it all in a short space of time, losing his cab licence in the process.

The cabmen of Dublin at that time were a close-knit group and they tended to look after one another in times of trouble. A cabman from New Street in the Liberties bought a horse from St Doolagh's Fair out in Coolock. The horse appeared to be in good condition, but a week later the beast went demented and jumped through a shop window in the city centre. The vet diagnosed that the horse had rabies, and it was put down. The cabman's colleagues got together and paid for the damage to the shop window and bought the driver a replacement for the horse. Despite their best efforts, the cabmen failed to trace the previous owner of the horse.

The practice of 'doing a runner' was just as prevalent in those times as it is today. 'Sconcing' the cabmen – running off without paying your fare – was a popular sport and it took place on a daily basis in the city. A favoured jumping-off spot for the 'sconcers' was the Four Courts, where they could make their escape through any one of a large number of doors.

TOMMY MOORE'S HOUSE

The poet Thomas Moore, son of a Dublin grocer and wine merchant, was born at 12 Aungier Street on 28 May 1779. He lived at this house from his birth until 1799, when he left to seek his fortune in London. Following Moore's death in 1852, Number 12 – described as 'a quaint gabled house' and a humble grocer's shop – was a place of great interest for visitors to Dublin, and even during those times there was a plaque on the wall of the house commemorating Moore's birth. There was also a bust in a niche at the front of the house, which was described as 'not being a work in the highest style of art', but better than the abomination that had been erected to Moore's memory in College Street. This statue, the work of the sculptor Christopher Moore of Gloucester Street, was erected in 1857 and was roundly condemned for its ugliness. One commentator called it 'this grotesque effigy of Thomas Moore' and 'an unfortunate memorial to the poet', while the *Irish Builder* described it as 'that hideous importation from London'. Incidentally, the old public toilets underneath this statue were christened – in the time-honoured fashion of the Dublin wit – 'The Meeting of the Waters'.

Controversy raged in Dublin during March and April 1866 over what was seen by the concerned citizens of Dublin as the desecration of 'Tommy Moore's house'. The house had undergone several renovations over the years but the hackles of conservationists were raised when the gable was removed and the old brick front of the house was covered with an ugly layer of cement. One letter-writer to the newspapers said: 'There is no language to describe the vulgar abomination of the whole thing.' Another called it a 'stupid, vulgar, uncalled-for destruction of our brick-and-mortar relics' and called for the perpetrator to be 'summarily condemned to have a very decided aggression made on a tender part of his body.' The situation was further exacerbated the following month when the new owner of the building, a Mr Hely, probably stung by the criticism, proceeded to remove the bust of Moore from the niche at the front of the house. Such was the outcry at this act of vandalism, however, that Hely was forced to replace the bust in its former position, claiming that he had never intended to remove it permanently.

Shortly before his death, Moore paid what proved to be his last visit to his former home in Aungier Street with his friend George Petrie, the famous actor and musician. As they stopped outside Number 12 in their carriage, Moore – with tears in his eyes – explained to Petrie that he wanted to see one last time 'the little gable window by which I penned my earliest verses, the Melodies.' Moore then returned to his home in Wiltshire, where he died on 25 February 1852.

THE SPA WELL

There are several theories in circulation regarding the true origin of the placename Templeogue in south Dublin. In the past it has been called *Teampall Aedog* (Aidan's Church) and *Teach Maelog*, meaning Maelog's house or church. One of the earliest references to Templeogue in south Dublin was in the *Crede Mihi*, a thirteenth-century church register. The church of Tachmelog was one of the churches listed in Dublin in 1275. The origins of this church were given a slightly confusing explanation by Archbishop Alen of Dublin in 1531. He said: 'The church of Tachmelogue was not a parochial church, but a chapel, annexed to the church of Kilmesantan which stood outside the boundaries of the Pale, which was erected within the boundaries of the Pale, on the city side of the Dodder, as being a more secure place for attendance at divine service during the then existing war; hence in the Irish tongue it is baptised rather as Temple Oyge because it is new.' The war referred to by the archbishop was the continuous conflict between the English settlers within the boundaries of the Pale and the O'Tooles living in the Dublin and Wicklow Mountains. According to the Reverend Myles Ronan, the Anglo-Normans were obliged to build the church at Tachmelog on the city side of the Dodder for the use of the local people, who were unable to use their church at Kilmesantan (now called St Anne's Church) because of the threat posed to them by the O'Tooles.

During the early years of the eighteenth century, the Spa

Well at Templeogue was a very fashionable meeting place for upwardly mobile Dubliners. The spa opened every year from April to September for those who wished to partake of its waters. If you couldn't face the long trek out to Templeogue, it was possible to get bottles of Templeogue mineral water delivered to your doorstep daily at the cost of two pence per bottle. During its heyday, the Spa Well became such an important event in Dublin's social calendar that it inspired the production of a weekly newspaper called the *Templeogue Intelligencer*, which was entirely devoted to the comings and goings at the well.

A copy of the *Dublin Gazette* in April 1732 advertised dancing at the Spawell House, which was then called the Domvile Arms and Three Tuns Tavern. The owner, Patrick Daniel, promised 'to give satisfaction to all persons who maketh use of the said water, there being a large room for the accommodation of gentlemen and ladies, as also good entertainment and attendance.' At the height of its popularity, in the 1730s, it was announced that coal had been discovered near the spa at Templeogue, but the colliery was abandoned soon after its opening.

In addition to its popularity as a health spa, Templeogue was also a popular venue for boxing and cock-fighting. A Dublin newspaper in 1744 carried the following advertisement for a 'cock-match', which was to take place on May Day of that year: 'a cock-match, between the County and City of Dublin, each side to shew thirty-one cocks; for two guineas a battle, and forty guineas the odd battle. To be fought in three days, wherein several gentlemen of the city and county are concerned . . . '

The spa went into decline in the late 1740s when the taste and appearance of the water deteriorated dramatically. Doctor John Rutty in his *History of the Mineral Waters of Ireland* (1757) examined the water and described it as 'limpid when fresh drawn, but grew white on an hour's standing: it left something unctuous on the sides of the glasses.' The only mineral water now available at the site is the bottled variety on sale behind the bar of the Spawell Leisure Centre, but unlike their counterparts of 270 years ago, I'm sure they don't do home deliveries.

THE OUZEL GALLEY

In 1695, the Dublin shipping company of Ferris, Twigg and Cash sent their merchant ship *The Ouzel Galley* on a trading mission to the port of Smyrna in Turkey. The ship, with a crew of thirty-seven and three officers, was commanded by Captain Eoghan Massey of Waterford. Three years passed and no news was heard from *The Ouzel Galley*. The ship's insurance underwriters decided that the ship had been lost at sea and, following arbitration, they agreed to settle Ferris, Twigg and Cash's claim in full.

Nearly five years to the day after its departure from Ringsend, *The Ouzel Galley*, to the amazement of all, arrived back in Dublin Bay with its crew intact and laden down with a cargo of riches. The official story at the time was that the ship had been captured by Algerian pirates who used it to terrorise the Mediterranean seas, although it was whispered in some quarters that Captain Massey might have been indulging in a spot of piracy himself. The official story went on to relate how the Irish crew, who had somehow been spared, managed to escape from captivity and regained control of the ship and the pirates' booty.

A legal wrangle developed between the ship's owners and the insurance company as to the ownership of the cargo. The insurance company claimed that they were the rightful owners as they had already settled the claim, while the ship's owners offered to pay the money back. The litigation dragged on in the courts for five years and the matter was settled only when the parties decided to abandon the costly legal process and went to arbitration instead. The arbitration committee, consisting of various Dublin merchants, soon decided, to the satisfaction of both parties, that the treasure should be donated to a fund to help merchants who had fallen on hard times. The arbitration scheme had worked so well that the merchants decided to form a permanent society with a view to settling commercial disputes without getting involved in expensive legal procedures. The committee decided to call themselves 'The Ouzel Galley Society'; membership was limited to forty, in honour of the original ship's crew.

The society adopted seafaring titles. Its first chairman, given the title of captain, was a former captain of *The Ouzel Galley*. Each member of the forty-strong society was given a title such as 'bosun', 'coxswain', 'gunner' or 'carpenter'. The members were often referred to as 'hands' in the minutes of the society, and a report of 1754 shows that the bosun was to be provided with a silver whistle for the purpose of piping the officers and hands to dinner at their three annual meetings. The Ouzel Galley Society held its meetings at the Commercial Buildings in Dame Street and operated from there until the early part of the nineteenth century. In 1888 the society was wound up by the courts and its funds were divided between several Dublin hospitals. A century earlier, most of the business of the society had been taken over by a new organisation known as the Committee of Merchants. This in turn became the Dublin Chamber of Commerce in 1783.

THE BLACK DOG

One of the most important markets in the old city of Dublin was the Cornmarket in High Street. As far back as the thirteenth century, corn, hides and wool were sold from Cornmarket, and many of the city's merchants lived in the area.

The market was in use until 1727, when it was transferred to Thomas Street. An interesting building that once existed in the area was Browne's Castle. The castle, which was really a tower, was named after Richard Browne, who had been Mayor of Dublin in 1614 and 1615. A room in the tower was used as a secret Mass-house in the days when the Penal Laws were in operation. The tower was afterwards converted for use as a tavern and later became known as the Black Dog Tavern. The tavern was owned by a man called Barton, who was sent for trial in 1641 for calling the Earl of Drogheda 'a cheating knave'.

From the early eighteenth century, the Black Dog was used as the main debtors' prison in Dublin. The prison contained about twenty beds, which the head warder rented out to prisoners for a fee of one shilling per night. Prisoners who could not afford to pay were dragged off to a damp, unlit dungeon that was invariably covered with raw sewage. This dungeon was also known as the nunnery because it was used to hold prostitutes who had been arrested by the parish watch.

John Gilbert's *History of the City of Dublin* carries a grim description of the Black Dog given by Sir Jeremiah Fitzpatrick in 1783. 'The Black Dog,' he wrote, 'is a most unwholesome situation in Newhall Market, surrounded with every exhalation necessary to promote putrefaction; it has neither yard or necessary, except in the cellar, to which none have access save those on the first floor.' Fitzpatrick also described visiting a room in the prison that contained 'five venereal female patients, and eight labouring under an inveterate itch.' In 1794, with the construction of a new jail at Green Street, the Black Dog ceased to function as a debtors' prison.

An interesting tale relating to the Black Dog was told in an issue of the *Dublin Penny Journal* in November 1832. The paper described how a creature who appeared in the form of a black pig had engaged in a reign of terror against the women of the city at the end of the eighteenth century.

The beast, known as the 'Dolocher', was commonly believed to be the spirit of a former inmate of the Black Dog named Olocher, who had been sentenced to death for murder and rape. He cheated the hangman, however, by committing suicide on the morning before his execution. Soon afterwards a warder at the Black Dog disappeared; it was rumoured that the Dolocher had murdered him. The Dolocher was finally caught and unmasked; it emerged that the 'black pig' was none other than the sentry who had disappeared from the Black Dog two years previously. He had apparently spread the rumour of the black pig himself and had used the resulting atmosphere of superstition and fear to embark on a crime spree.

SELECT BIBLIOGRAPHY

BOOKS

Andrews, C. S. *Dublin Made Me*. Cork: Mercier Press, 1979.

Appleyard, D. *Green Fields Gone Forever: The Story of the Coolock and Artane Area*. Dublin: 1985.

Ball, F. E. *A History of the County Dublin*. Dublin: Alexander Thom, 1906.

Barrington, J. *Personal Sketches of His Own Times*. 3 Vols. London: 1830–2.

Boylan, H. *A Dictionary of Irish Biography*. Dublin: Gill and Macmillan, 1978.

Bradley, J. (ed.) *Viking Dublin Exposed*. Dublin: O'Brien Press, 1984.

Burton, N. J. *Letters from Harold's Cross 1850*. Dublin: Carrig Books, 1979.

Chart, D. A. *Dublin*. London: J. M. Dent, 1907.

Cosgrave, D. *North Dublin City and Environs*. Dublin: Four Courts Press, 1909.

Craig, M. *Dublin 1660–1860*. Dublin: 1969

D'Alton, J. *The History of the County Dublin*. Dublin: Hodges and Smith, 1838.

De Courcy, J. W. *The Liffey in Dublin*. Dublin: Gill and Macmillan, 1996.

Fagan, P. *The Second City, Portrait of Dublin 1700–60*. Dublin: Branar, 1986.

Fayle, H. and A. Newham. *The Dublin & Blessington Steam Tramway*. Surrey: Oakwood Press, 1963.

Fitzpatrick, W. J. *The Sham Squire and the Informers of 1798*. London: 1866.

Gilbert, J. T. A *History of the City of Dublin*. 3 vols. Vol. 1, Dublin: James McGlashan, 1854; Vols 2 & 3, Dublin: McGlashan and Gill, 1859.

Gilbert, J. T. (ed.) and Lady Gilbert. *Calendar of Ancient Records of Dublin*, 19 Vols. Dublin: Joseph Dollard, 1889–1944.

Gilligan, H. A. *History of the Port of Dublin*. Dublin: 1988.

Haliday, C. *The Scandinavian Kingdom of Dublin*. Dublin: Alex Thom, 1881.

Handcock, W. D. *The History and Antiquities of Tallaght*. Dublin: Tower Books (reprint), 1976.

Harris, W. *History of the Antiquities of the City of Dublin*. Dublin: L. Flynn, 1766.

Harrison, W. *Memorable Dublin Houses*. Dublin: 1890.

Henry, B. *Dublin Hanged*. Dublin: Irish Academic Press, 1994.

Joyce, Weston St John. *The Neighbourhood of Dublin*. Dublin, 1921.

Leeson, M., (ed. Lyons, M.) *Memoirs of Mrs Margaret Leeson*. Dublin: Lilliput Press (reprint), 1995.

Lewis, S. A *Topographical Dictionary of Ireland*. London: 1837.

Little, G. A. *Malachi Horan Remembers*. Dublin: 1944.

Maxwell, C. *Dublin Under the Georges*. London: George Harrap, 1946.

McCall, P. J. *In the Shadow of St Patrick's*. Dublin: 1894.

McCready, C. T. *Dublin Street Names, Dated and Explained*. Dublin: Hodges Figgis, 1892.

McGregor, J. J. *New Picture of Dublin: Comprehending a History of the City*. Dublin: John Allen and John James McGregor, 1821.

McLoughlin, A. *Guide to Historic Dublin*. Dublin: Gill and Macmillan, 1979.

O'Keefe, J. *Recollections*. London: 1826.

Peter, A. *Sketches of Old Dublin*. Dublin: 1907.

Sheridan, P. H. *The Personal Memoirs of P. H. Sheridan*. New York: Da Capo Press, 1992.

Walsh, J. E. *Sketches of Ireland Sixty Years Ago*. London: 1847.

Webb, J. J. *The Guilds of Dublin*. London: Benn, 1929.

Whaley, Buck and Sir E. Sullivan (ed.) *Memoirs*. London: 1906.

NEWSPAPERS, PERIODICALS, JOURNALS

The *Dublin Evening Post*
Dublin Historical Record
Dublin Courant
Dublin Penny Journal
Dublin University Magazine
The *Evening Herald*
Faulkner's Dublin Journal
The *Freeman's Journal*
The *Gentleman's Magazine*
The *Hibernian Journal*
The *Irish Builder and Engineer*
Irish Ecclesiastical Record
The *Irish Independent*
The *Irish Press*
The *Irish Times*
The *Irish Worker*
Journal of the Royal Society of Antiquaries of Ireland
Saunders' Newsletter